The Visual MBA

The Visual MBA

Two Years of Business School Packed into One Priceless Book of Pure Awesomeness

Jason Barron, MBA

HARVEST
An Imprint of WILLIAM MORROW

First Mariner Books edition 2020
Copyright © 2019 by Jason Barron

Library of Congress Cataloging-in-Publication Data
Names: Barron, Jason, author.
Title: The visual MBA : two years of business school packed into one priceless book of
pure awesomeness / Jason Barron.
Description: Boston : HarperCollins Publishers, 2019. |
Includes bibliographical references.
Identifiers: LCCN 2018051342 (print) | LCCN 2019000388 (ebook) |
ISBN 978-0-358-02539-9 (ebook) | ISBN 978-0-358-02395-1 (hardback) |
ISBN 978-0-358-34364-6 (pbk.)
Subjects: LCSH: Business education. | Strategic planning. | Management. |
BISAC: BUSINESS & ECONOMICS / Education. | BUSINESS & ECONOMICS / Careers /
General. | HUMOR / Topic / Business & Professional.
Classification: LCC HF1106 (ebook) | LCC HF1106 .B28 2019 (print) |
DDC 658—dc23
LC record available at https://lccn.loc.gov/2018051342

Printed in Canada
24 TC 10 9 8 7 6 5 4 3

To Jackie, Josh, James, Jonah, Josie & Junie
(My whole world)

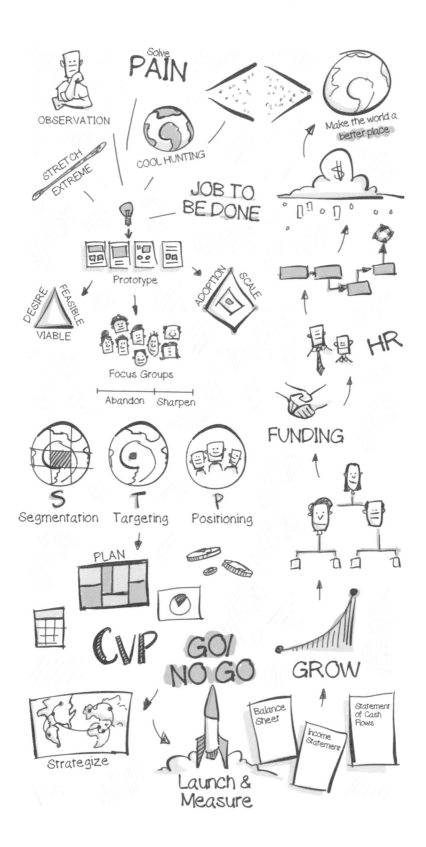

Contents

Preface

In short, this book contains two long years of business school, all neatly packaged into one highly illustrated volume.

Experts tell us that 60% of people are visual learners and—let's face it—beyond that, 100% of people don't want to read boring stuff. Now, with this book you can understand faster, absorb better, and recall quicker the biggest and most useful ideas that you would learn from studying for a Master's of Business Administration degree.

A quick word about the illustrations that follow. Years ago Mike Rohde coined the term "sketchnotes," and I've been a fan ever since. Rather than taking extensive linear notes that no one (including yourself) will ever read again, I felt that simply capturing the main points visually would create a much more interesting and useful resource for later consumption. As they say, "A picture is worth 1,000 words."

At the beginning of my MBA studies, I took on the crazy goal to try and create "sketchnotes" throughout the entire program. And something unexpected happened. For a class full of extremely smart people (all smarter than me), I was surprised at the high level of interest they had in my visual notes as I went along.

What you have in front of you is the end product of all my sketchnotes as I attended the BYU Marriott School of Business. Whether you've never been to business school (and never will), or have already attended, or are in a current MBA program yourself, I created this book with you in mind. Each chapter is based upon traditional business school classes, and is packed with concepts that are accompanied with a written narrative to help you better understand it all.

Feel free to skim, jump, or dive through the content any way you want. The only rules are to have fun, to be curious, and to discover on your own. You will be glad you did.

Now sit back, relax, and enjoy all the knowledge soaking into your (genius) brain.

Author's Note

You're smart: I just spent 86 class days, endured 516 hours of various lectures, completed mountains of homework, and shelled out tens of thousands of dollars in tuition fees, and you can benefit from it all with this book at a fraction of the cost in the comfort of your own home. Nice business decision.

My name is Jason Barron, and I'm a designer. I've always been doodling, sometimes when I shouldn't — like in class as a kid. Fast-forward 20 years and not much has changed. Except that I decided to put my lifelong doodling habit to work when I received an MBA from a top 40 business school, Brigham Young University.

Each class period I would sketchnote what the professor was saying, including key thoughts during class, and from reading assignments. I would capture the essence of what was being taught and then I would distill the complex lectures into simplified concepts.

The end result is this book, which is worth more than gold. It is the goose that keeps on giving luscious golden eggs in the form of paper pages. Save yourself countless hours and read this book in a fun, fast, and memorable way. (You will love it, and if not you can always re-gift it!)

You ready to get smarter? (If that's even possible, you genius you.) Let's get to it!

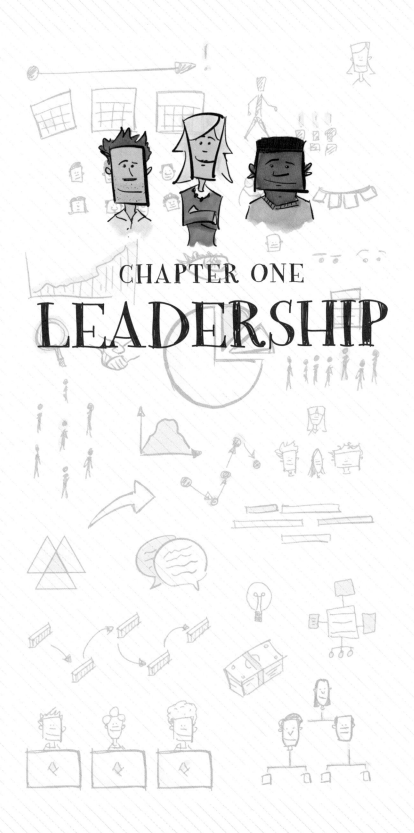

CHAPTER ONE

LEADERSHIP

Leadership is more than management. It's about inspiring change and improving results through who you are and how you motivate others.

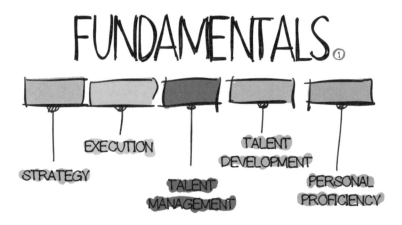

Strategy
Creating the future vision and positioning the company for ongoing success

Execution
Building organizational systems to deliver results based on the strategy

Talent Management
Motivating, engaging, and communicating with employees

Talent Development
Grooming employees for future leadership

Personal Proficiency
Acting with integrity, exercising social and emotional intelligence, making bold decisions, and engendering trust

WHAT IS YOUR LEADERSHIP
BRAND?

When people see you, what do they think/feel about you? That's your brand.

5 STEPS
to building a brand that
GETS RESULTS

1) Nail down the results you want to achieve over the next 12 months

Make sure to consider the interests of your customers, investors, employees, and the organization as a whole.

2) Decide what you want to be known for

Looking at your results, how do you want to be perceived? Pick six descriptors that you want to be known for. Example: Humble, Optimistic, Dedicated, etc.

3) Combine to define

Combine your six descriptors into three two-word phrases. Example: Humbly Optimistic, Selflessly Dedicated, etc.

4) Create your leadership brand statement & test it

I want to be known for being (three phrases) so that I can deliver _____. Then ask, "Does this best represent me?" "Does it create value for my stakeholders?" "Are there any risks?"

5) Make it real

Share your brand with others and ask if they feel it aligns with how you truly behave. Make adjustments. Most importantly, your brand is a promise — so make it real and DELIVER.

7 FIRST IMPRESSION TAKES SECONDS ③

① Pre-Adjust your ATTITUDE

④ Make EYE CONTACT

② Adjust your POSTURE

⑤ Raise your EYEBROWS

⑥ Shake HANDS

③ SMILE

⑦ LEAN IN

Move your employees from being disengaged to engaged with autonomy, mastery, and purpose. Give them the freedom to be creative, to be good at what they do, and to have a purpose behind their work.

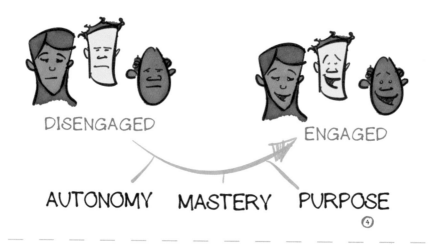

DISENGAGED

ENGAGED

AUTONOMY   MASTERY   PURPOSE

If you want to be happy in your job you need to hit the sweet spot. You need a balance of competence (really good at something), passion (need I say more?), and opportunity (there is a market need).

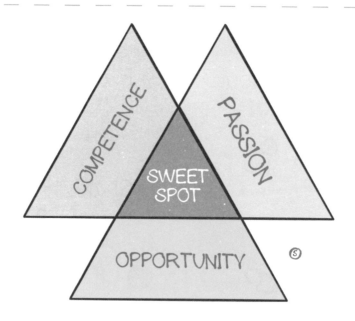

COMPETENCE

PASSION

SWEET SPOT

OPPORTUNITY

CHANGE THE CONTEXT OF WHERE PEOPLE WORK
AND PEOPLE WILL CHANGE

WHAT IS THE "SMELL" OF THE PLACE? ⑥

Although it is hard to change people, nothing changes people faster than changing their environment. Their environment then shapes the culture.

Look around. What is the "smell" of the place they work? Is it stuffy? Compliance driven? Is it quiet? Are there cubicles that block them from others? Does it feel dead? That is your culture. Change that and people change along with your culture.

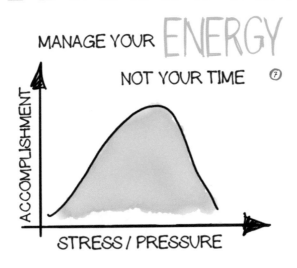

MANAGE YOUR ENERGY
NOT YOUR TIME ⑦

ACCOMPLISHMENT

STRESS / PRESSURE

Some stress is helpful to increase performance but there comes a point where performance drops. Make sure to take breaks, exercise, and relax to maintain performance.

4C's OF TEAM PERFORMANCE ⑧

① CONTEXT

WHAT IS THE ENVIRONMENT?
WHAT IS THE TONE?

REWARDS

GOALS

CONTEXT includes the reward system, goals, culture, tone, and environment that the team will be working in.

---

② COMPOSITION

SKILLS & PERSONALITY

COMPOSITION includes who is on the team and their skills and personalities to get the job done. This is where hiring the right people who mesh with the team is critical.

③ COMPETENCIES

GOAL SETTING & ACHIEVEMENT

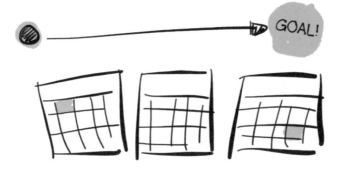

COMPETENCIES includes having the right people whose combined skill can solve the problem. It's about setting the right goal and leveraging the team's skill to achieve it.

④ CHANGE

ADAPTABILITY

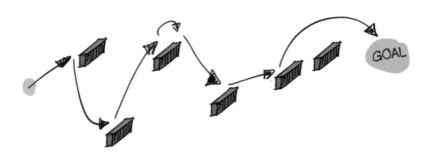

CHANGE includes the team's ability to adapt to rapidly changing circumstances while working towards the goal.

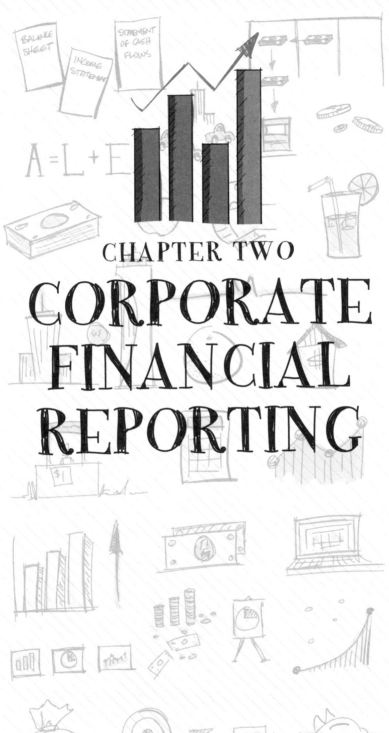

CHAPTER TWO

CORPORATE FINANCIAL REPORTING

Accounting is the language of business. Unless you are keeping track of how your company is doing, you won't know how to improve it. Everything in this course revolves around these three financial statements.

You are the new CEO .... of a lemonade stand. You need a loan of $50 (liability) to buy some assets. You purchase a stand for $20 and have $30 left over.

BALANCE SHEET
(STATEMENT OF NET WORTH)

SNAPSHOT IN TIME COMPRISED OF:

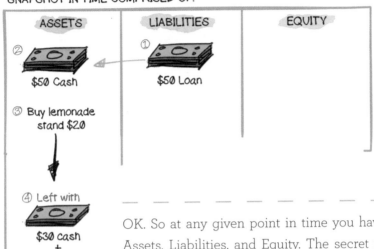

ASSETS	LIABILITIES	EQUITY
② $50 Cash	① $50 Loan	
③ Buy lemonade stand $20		

④ Left with

$30 cash
+

Lemonade

Worth $20

OK. So at any given point in time you have Assets, Liabilities, and Equity. The secret is, Assets = Liabilities + Equity. That's called the "Accounting Equation." Your loan was $50 (Liability), you used it to buy a stand for $20 (Asset), and have $30 cash (Asset). You have $50 debt (Liability) and $50 of assets. A = L + E.

ACCOUNTING EQUATION

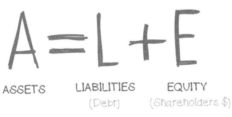

$$A = L + E$$

ASSETS	LIABILITIES	EQUITY
	(Debt)	(Shareholders $)

$90

BAM! You just sold $90 worth of lemonade. Nicely done. Your balance sheet looks something like this now.

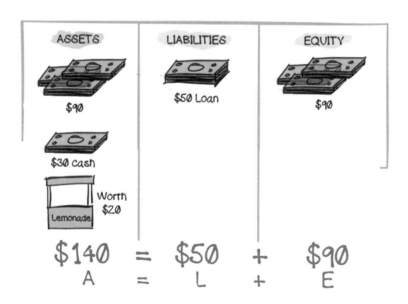

ASSETS	LIABILITIES	EQUITY
$90	$50 Loan	$90
$30 cash		
Lemonade Worth $20		

$$\underset{A}{\$140} = \underset{L}{\$50} + \underset{E}{\$90}$$

A balance sheet is a snapshot in time and is a good indicator of your net worth as a business. Now let's jump into your income statement.

INCOME STATEMENT
AKA - "Profit & Loss" or "Earnings"

(Sales)
REVENUE - EXPENSES = NET PROFIT

REVENUE

SALES	$90
COST OF GOODS SOLD	$20
GROSS PROFIT	$70

$70 / $90 = 77% (Gross profit margin)

OPERATING EXPENSES

ADMINISTRATIVE	$3
OPERATING INCOME	$67
(aka EBIT)	

$67 / $90 = 74% (Operating profit margin)

REMAINING EXPENSES

TAXES	$2
INTEREST	$1
NET PROFIT	$64

$64 / $90 = 71% (Net profit margin)

Sure. You sold $90 but the cups, sugar, and lemons cost $20. Your gross profit is $70. You also had to pay for some administrative overhead. That left you with $67 operating income or EBIT (Earnings Before Interest & Taxes). You then need to take out interest and taxes, which leaves you with a net profit of $64.

STATEMENT OF CASH FLOWS

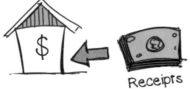

Receipts

Payments

THEY CAN BE EITHER:

① OPERATING ACTIVITIES ~~~~ NET CASH FROM
  + SALE OF GOODS   OPERATIONS IS THE
  − INVENTORY PURCHASES   BOTTOM LINE OF
  − WAGES PAID   CASH FLOW STATEMENT
  − ETC.

② INVESTING ACTIVITIES
  + SALE OF ASSETS
  − PURCHASING OF ASSETS

CASH IS AN
UNPRODUCTIVE
ASSET

③ FINANCING ACTIVITIES
  + ISSUANCE OF STOCK
  + BORROWING
  − LOAN PAYMENTS

USE IT!
TO BUY ASSETS

PLANS ALWAYS APPEAR DURING
A CRISIS, BUT ARE NEEDED
BEFORE

GOAL ➡ PLAN ➡ EVALUATE ➡ ADJUST

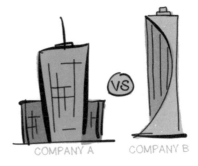

COMPANY A   COMPANY B

DIAGNOSE or COMPARE

COMMON SIZED financial statements are a great way to figure out how you are doing over time, or to compare one company in a similar industry with another. All you do is divide everything by sales to see where any differences are.

		Year 2	Year 1
REVENUE			
SALES	$90	100%	67%
COST OF GOODS SOLD	$20	(22%)	(33%)
GROSS PROFIT	$70	78%	33%
OPERATING EXPENSES			
ADMINISTRATIVE	$3	(3%)	(2%)
OPERATING INCOME (aka EBIT)	$67	74%	31%
REMAINING EXPENSES			
TAXES	$2	(2%)	(1%)
INTEREST	$1	(1%)	(1%)
NET PROFIT	$64	71%	28%

PRO FORMA

Pro forma is just a fancy way of saying "what the future could look like." It is forecasting based on an increase in sales. Look at your financial statement and everything on it that is dependent on sales. In this case, let's say COST OF GOODS SOLD (COGS) and ADMINISTRATIVE expenses both increase with sales.

If sales increased by 20%, what would our net profit be? Look at the previous page and see that COGS was 22% of sales, and your administrative expense was 3%. When increasing $90 by 20% ($108), you then figure out what 22% and 3% (COGS and administrative, respectively) of $108 are.

REVENUE		Pro Forma
SALES	$90	$108
COST OF GOODS SOLD	$20	$23.76
GROSS PROFIT	$70	$84.24

OPERATING EXPENSES		
ADMINISTRATIVE	$3	$3.24
OPERATING INCOME (aka EBIT)	$67	$81

REMAINING EXPENSES		
TAXES	$2	$2
INTEREST	$1	$1
NET PROFIT	$64	$78

FINANCIAL RATIOS

Financial ratios are a great way to compare how you are doing over time, to diagnose any issues, or to see how one company in a similar industry stacks up against another. **Here are some of the most common.**

Debt-to-equity
Financial leverage: How much debt is used to finance your assets.

Total Liabilities / Shareholder Equity

Current Ratio
Liquidity: Your company's ability to pay back short-term obligations. The higher the ratio, the higher the capability.

Current Assets / Current Liabilities

Return on Equity
Profit generated with money invested by shareholders.

Net Income / Shareholder's Equity
(%)

Net Profit Margin
Efficiency at cost control in converting revenue into profit. The higher the number, the better.

Net Profit / Net Sales

DUPONT FRAMEWORK

This is a combo-equation that shows some of the strengths and weaknesses of the company and how they affect the return on equity.

$$ROE = \frac{\text{Net Income}}{\text{Sales}}$$

$$\times$$

$$\frac{\text{Sales}}{\text{Assets}}$$

$$\times$$

$$\frac{\text{Assets}}{\text{Equity}}$$

How Shares Work

When starting your lemonade stand you established that there would be 100 shares. You took on a business partner and now each of you owns 20 shares. Where the business stands, you now both own 20% of the business. Your company is worth $204 now, so how much is each share worth?

Company worth: $204 ($64 net income + $140 assets)
$204/100 (shares) = $2.04 per share

Each owns

 20 x $2.04 = $40.80

CHAPTER THREE

ENTREPRENEURIAL MANAGEMENT

Entrepreneurial Management is about solving unknown problems (pain) with unknown solutions (innovation). The key to solving uncertainty is by identifying pain, and the key to finding the right solution is by experimentation.

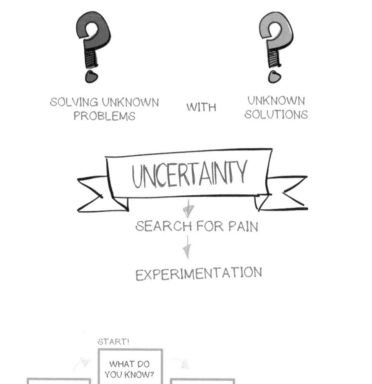

SOLVING UNKNOWN PROBLEMS   WITH   UNKNOWN SOLUTIONS

UNCERTAINTY

SEARCH FOR PAIN

EXPERIMENTATION

START!

WHAT DO YOU KNOW?

CONCLUSIONS

WHAT DON'T YOU KNOW?

EXPERIMENT

RESULTS

DESIGN EXPERIMENT

CONDUCT EXPERIMENT

"ENLIGHTENED TRIAL & ERROR SUCCEEDS OVER THE PLANNING OF THE LONE GENIUS."

- PETER SKILLMAN PRES. OF IDEO

Run your experiment. Start with what you know. Then, what is unknown (question or hypothesis)? Design your experiment, conduct, learn, and around and around you go until you have a successful product.

Your idea needs to be desirable, feasible, and viable. If any of those are missing, your product is limited out of the gate.

PAIN. The essential ingredient for innovation. Look around for makeshift solutions that people have created in absence of a product. The deeper the pain, the greater the opportunity.

ANY PROBLEM OR UNMET NEED THAT
CUSTOMERS WILL SPEND THEIR TIME
OR MONEY TO SOLVE.

ALWAYS LOOK FOR DEEP PAIN

Gaining broad adoption takes a balance of price, benefits, ease of use, and ease of purchase. If there are strengths in all these areas, the percentage of adoption will be much greater.

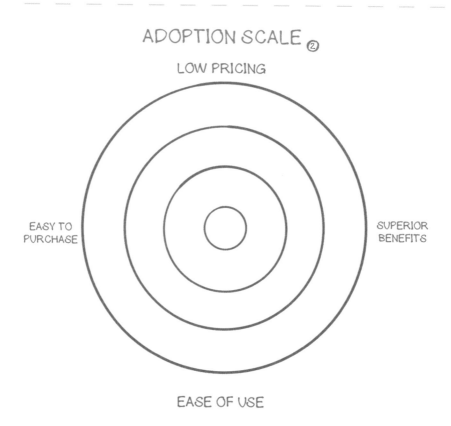

ADOPTION SCALE ②

LOW PRICING

EASY TO PURCHASE

SUPERIOR BENEFITS

EASE OF USE

PRODUCT A   PRODUCT B   PRODUCT C

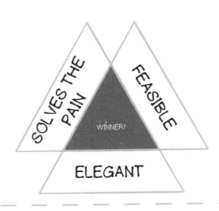

"SIMPLICITY IS THE
ULTIMATE SOPHISTICATION."
- Steve Jobs

"When you start looking at a problem and it seems really simple with all these simple solutions, you don't really understand the complexity of the problem .... Then you get into the problem, and you see it's really complicated. And you come up with all these convoluted solutions .... That's ... where most people stop .... But the really great person will keep going and find the key .... The underlying principle of the problem. And come up with a beautiful elegant solution that works." — Steve Jobs (quoted by Steven Levy, The Perfect Thing). ③

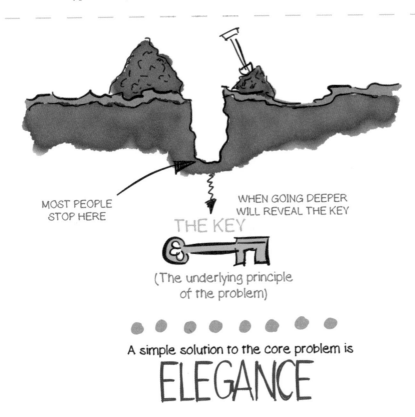

MOST PEOPLE
STOP HERE

WHEN GOING DEEPER
WILL REVEAL THE KEY

THE KEY

(The underlying principle
of the problem)

A simple solution to the core problem is
ELEGANCE

NOT ALL PAIN IS WORTH SOLVING

SPEND YOUR ENERGY ON THE
MOST PROFITABLE
(BIGGEST MOUNTAINS)

You may have the best idea for something that isn't all that profitable or that big of a pain for people. Find the areas of unresolved pain that are also as profitable as possible.

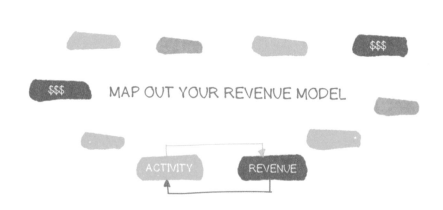

$$$

$$$ MAP OUT YOUR REVENUE MODEL

ACTIVITY   REVENUE

Maximize your revenue by mapping it out. Identify which activities and customers it is coming from. Also look at reducing any friction points for receiving the revenue.

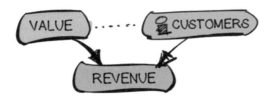

Pricing is one of the most critical aspects of creating new products. Priced too low and you leave money on the table. Priced too high, you lose customers. The trick is finding ways to price it just right. One of the best ways to shed light on the right price is by surveying customers.

ASK: HOW MUCH WOULD YOU BE
     WILLING TO PAY FOR THIS?

HOW MANY TIMES PER (MONTH, YEAR)
WOULD YOU PAY x?

2.00	5.00	10.00
10	6	1
$20	$30	$10

WINNER!
PRICE @ $5.00

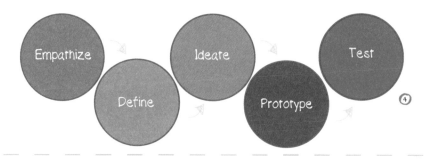

Stanford's d.school came up with this brilliant process for innovation. This is a rapid way you can discover new innovations and validate them.

When Walt Disney was building his theme parks he would get down on one knee to see the park from a child's perspective. Empathy is the critical first step to understanding your customer's world and building products or experiences that meet their needs.

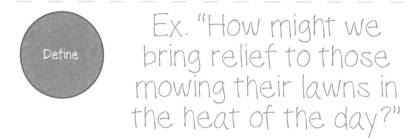

Ex. "How might we bring relief to those mowing their lawns in the heat of the day?"

Based on what you learned through empathy, what is the problem you will focus on solving? Craft an actionable problem statement.

Now take what you learned with the problem in mind and start coming up with ideas. The more ideas, the better.

Filter your ideas down and build a prototype. This can be out of duct tape and paper. This prototype is only to validate your idea and to test it with people. It doesn't need to be fancy.

Find some people who fit your target, and test your prototype. What worked? What didn't? What did you learn? Take those learnings and go back to Ideate -> Prototype -> Test again.

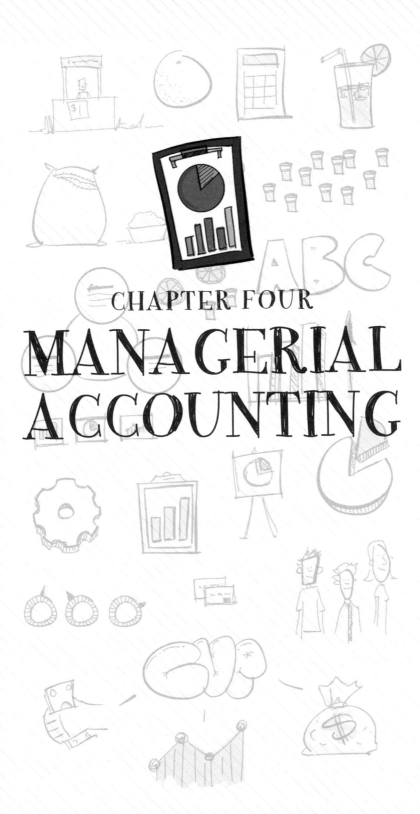

CHAPTER FOUR

MANAGERIAL ACCOUNTING

Managerial accounting is for internal use in order to inform decisions, unlike corporate accounting, which is for external use (investors, etc.).

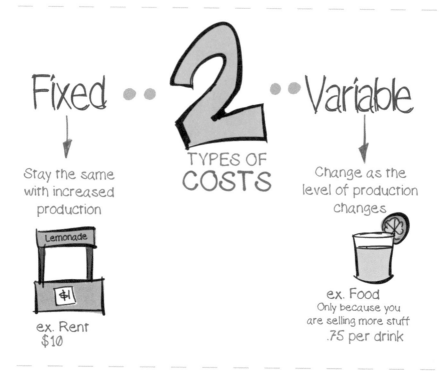

Fixed ··

TYPES OF
COSTS

··Variable

Stay the same
with increased
production

ex. Rent
$10

Change as the
level of production
changes

ex. Food
Only because you
are selling more stuff
.75 per drink

Lemonade
$1

You track fixed and variable costs separately and don't unitize them as they are fundamentally different. $10 rent is fixed, whereas the more lemonade you sell, the more the costs (and profit) increase.

Cost   Volume   Profit

CVP analysis sounds fancy, but it's simple. You simply take what your sales price is, subtract the per-unit cost, and then multiply it by the volume you anticipate selling. This helps you understand how changes in cost will affect operating and net income.

Revenue - Cost = Contribution Margin
(Sales)

"Contribution margin" sounds fancy too, but it's just what you have left over per unit after subtracting the cost to "contribute" to paying your fixed cost (in this case, the sweet lemonade stand).

So, we sell our lemonade at $1. Sugar and the lemons cost .75 per cup. So . . . . we have a .25 profit that can "contribute" to paying our $10 fixed cost for rent.

$1 - .75 = .25

Contribution Margin

Use it to "contribute" to your fixed costs

$10 Rent/mo
(Fixed Cost)

Here is where it gets cool. You are planning out your business and you think, "Gee, my rent costs $10, my lemonade sells for $1, and I make a .25 profit. How many cups do I need to sell in order to cover rent?"

$$\$10 \ / \ (\$1 - .75) = 40 \text{ Cups need to be sold in order to break even}$$

Sweet! Now you're movin'. If you sold $160 worth of lemonade, your variable cost (cost per unit multiplied by the number sold) would be $120 (.75x160). Apply the remainder ($40 profit) to your fixed cost and you just made a $30 profit. That's how it's done!

TODAY I SOLD 160 CUPS!

$$(\$160 - \$120) - \$10 = \$30 \text{ profit}$$

160 x $1   160 x $.75   Fixed

GOALS

I want to make $1,000 in profit a month

$$\frac{\text{Fixed Cost} + \text{Goal}}{\text{Contribution Margin}}$$

$$\frac{\$10 + 1000}{.25} = 4{,}040 \text{ cups!}$$

ACTIVITY   BASED   COSTING

USE ABC TO UNDERSTAND OVERHEAD COSTS

- ELECTRICITY - $5
- MAINTENANCE - $2   } $8 overhead
- CLEANERS - $1
- ETC...

Activity Based Costing is important in understanding the overhead costs that happen in the normal course of business. Analyzing these will help you know which activities are worth continuing by surfacing what they really cost.

THE MANAGEMENT PROCESS ①

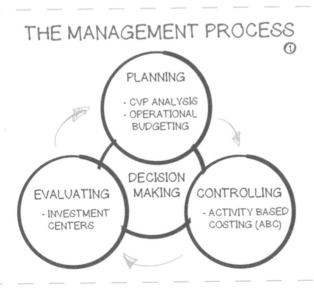

PLANNING
- CVP ANALYSIS
- OPERATIONAL BUDGETING

DECISION MAKING

EVALUATING
- INVESTMENT CENTERS

CONTROLLING
- ACTIVITY BASED COSTING (ABC)

The Management Process is fairly straightforward. Planning, Controlling, and Evaluating will help inform your decisions.

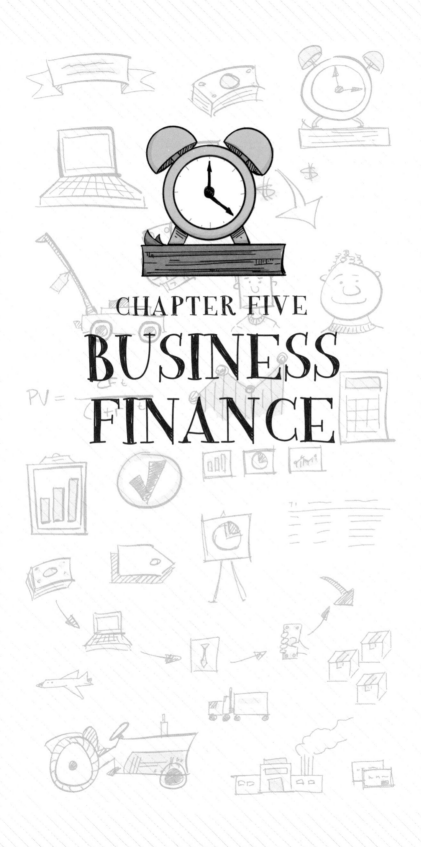

CHAPTER FIVE
BUSINESS FINANCE

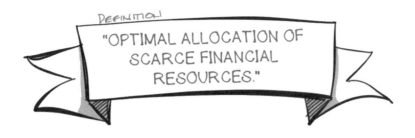

DEFINITION

"OPTIMAL ALLOCATION OF
SCARCE FINANCIAL
RESOURCES."

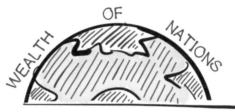

OF

WEALTH   NATIONS

f(Natural resources, labor, innovation, financial capital)

Suboptimal procurement, deployment, and distribution of financial capital lead to the suboptimal use of natural resources, labor, and innovation in an economy. We are focused in this course around optimal DEPLOYMENT.

OPTIMAL

DEPLOYMENT

HOW SHOULD WE USE IT?

① GO/NO GO DECISIONS

② ASSET PURCHASES & SALES

③ OPERATIONAL EFFICIENCIES

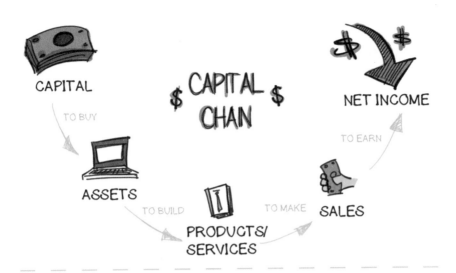

CAPITAL

$ CAPITAL $
CHAIN

NET INCOME

TO BUY

TO EARN

ASSETS

TO BUILD

TO MAKE

SALES

PRODUCTS/
SERVICES

The capital chain starts with capital that is used to buy assets to create products that generate sales and increase net income. Financial ratios can help analyze how efficiently we are managing the capital chain.

THE VALUE OF AN ASSET IS DRIVEN BY THE UTILITY OF AN ASSET

WHAT ABOUT CASH?

UTILITY
IS FUTURE
CASH FLOWS

SITTING IN A BANK IS
WORTHLESS

All goods and services are influenced by time. The utility of cash is future cash flows, and those cash flows are influenced by time. $100 now vs. receiving in 5 years changes the value. Next we will look at how this can be calculated.

TIME VALUE OF MONEY

HOW MUCH WOULD YOU GIVE

NOW

FOR A PROMISE OF $1,000

IN 5 YEARS

LESS THAN $1,000, THAT'S FOR SURE!

SO... HOW MUCH?

The next part seems intimidating but it's really cake. You know intuitively that getting $1,000 now isn't the same as getting it in 5 years. There is a lot you could have done with that cash (invest it in the stock market, etc.). So, what is $1,000 in 5 years really worth right now?

You could invest it somewhere else and get a return, but you also need to factor in some risks in case someone won't pay up. Those are accounted for in the "discount rate" (4% in this case, but it can be whatever you want).

1. $$PV = \frac{CF_t}{(1 + r)^t}$$

2. $$PV = \frac{\$1,000}{(1 + .04)^5}$$

3. $$PV = \$821.93$$

I'll give you $821.93 (How much it's worth)

OR! If you give less ($700), you would have a positive net present value $121.93

Let's break this beast down. PV, that's what you are trying to figure out (worth today). CFt — that's just the lump sum in the future, so $1,000 in this case. (1+r), that's just adding 1 + 4%. t — That's just 5 (5 years). BAM! Now you know what it's worth.

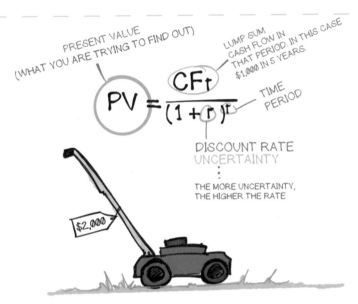

PRESENT VALUE
(WHAT YOU ARE TRYING TO FIND OUT)

LUMP SUM
CASH FLOW IN
THAT PERIOD, IN THIS CASE
$1,000 IN 5 YEARS.

$$PV = \frac{CF_t}{(1+r)^t}$$

TIME
PERIOD

DISCOUNT RATE
UNCERTAINTY
.
.
.
THE MORE UNCERTAINTY,
THE HIGHER THE RATE

$2,000

SHOULD I BUY THIS LAWNMOWER FOR MY LANDSCAPING BUSINESS?

(2,000)

YEAR	YEARLY CASH FLOWS	PRESENT VALUE OF THE CASH FLOWS
1	1,000	$1,000 / (1 + 10\%)^1 = 909.09$
2	1,000	$1,000 / (1 + 10\%)^2 = 826.45$
3	1,000	$1,000 / (1 + 10\%)^3 = 751.31$
4	1,000	$1,000 / (1 + 10\%)^4 = 683.01$
5	1,000	$1,000 / (1 + 10\%)^5 = 620.92$

BUY

$3,790.79

(2,000)

$1,790.79

Armed with this power, you can tell whether or not a $2,000 mower is really worth the investment when you look at the cash flow it will bring in down the road.

CHAPTER SIX

MARKETING

Marketing is about promoting products and services. First rule — you don't try to serve everybody. You segment the available market, then target a segment, then position the product.

SEGMENT

POSITION

Position the product around what your target values

How do we position to touch hearts and minds?

Who COULD we exchange with?

TARGET

Who SHOULD we exchange with?

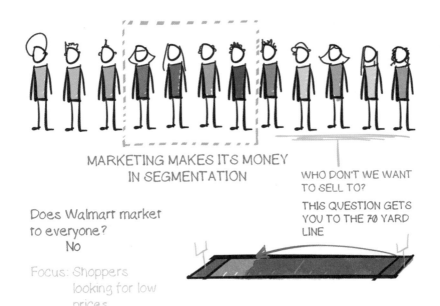

MARKETING MAKES ITS MONEY
IN SEGMENTATION

WHO DON'T WE WANT
TO SELL TO?

Does Walmart market
to everyone?
No

THIS QUESTION GETS
YOU TO THE 70 YARD
LINE

Focus: Shoppers
looking for low
prices

WHO is your customer, and who IS NOT?

This is one of the most difficult steps in marketing. We want to sell to everybody but if we try that, we end up watering down our product messaging and it doesn't appeal to anyone. Get focused on who your target is and then position it from there.

Segmentation and targeting can be approached like this: As much as we would love the whole world to be our customer, it ain't gonna happen. Instead, look at the potential market, then the actual available market. Segment it and target the most valuable potential customers.

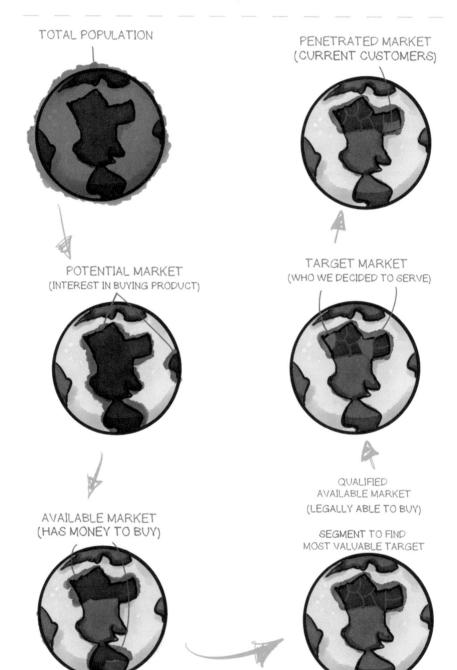

TOTAL POPULATION

PENETRATED MARKET
(CURRENT CUSTOMERS)

POTENTIAL MARKET
(INTEREST IN BUYING PRODUCT)

TARGET MARKET
(WHO WE DECIDED TO SERVE)

AVAILABLE MARKET
(HAS MONEY TO BUY)

QUALIFIED
AVAILABLE MARKET
(LEGALLY ABLE TO BUY)

SEGMENT TO FIND
MOST VALUABLE TARGET

Laddering is a great way to map out your product, see how it connects with your target, and decide how to use that to create marketing materials.

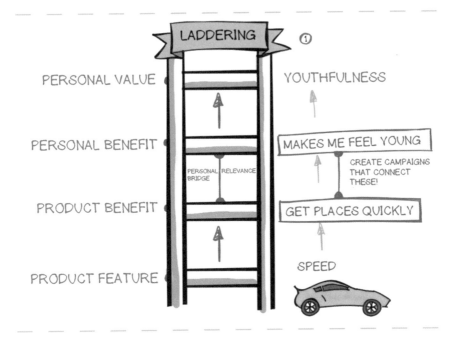

Ask your biggest fans what they like (a particular feature), why they like it (product benefit), why that matters (personal benefit), and how that connects to a high-level personal value. The link between the product and personal benefit is where the magic happens.

Now you can position your marketing materials through the love group's eyes, while targeting the swing group to gain new customers.

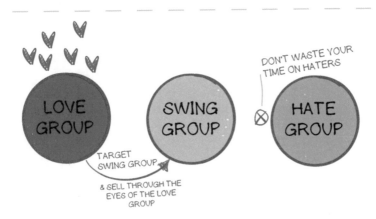

Let's take our lemonade business and do some love group interviews. You should end up with a laddering "Hierarchical Value Map"① like the one below. When you notice patterns of responses you can bold those lines and focus on the ones that are on the personal relevance bridge.

"What about our lemonade do you love?"

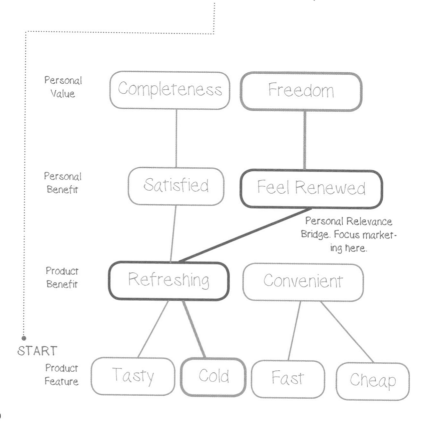

Personal Value	Completeness / Freedom
Personal Benefit	Satisfied / Feel Renewed
	Personal Relevance Bridge. Focus marketing here.
Product Benefit	Refreshing / Convenient
START	
Product Feature	Tasty / Cold / Fast / Cheap

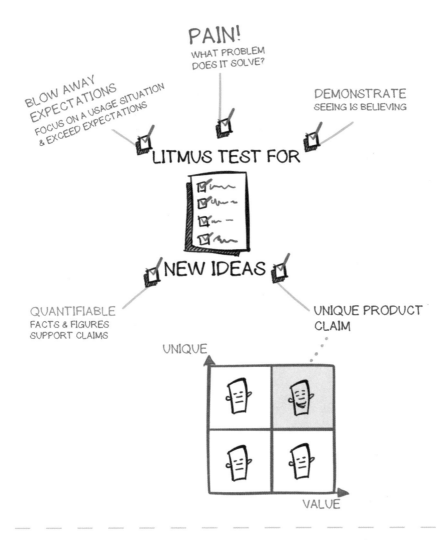

When working through new ideas and marketing them, make sure you can pass the litmus test above. The more of these dimensions you have, the sharper your angle. Also, a good way to find out if you have a good idea is to ask if people would buy it and for how much.

ASK

"On a scale of 1–10, how likely are you to buy this?"

ANYTHING OVER 7.5 IS A POTENTIAL WOW

BRAND

THE SUM TOTAL OF THE
IMPRESSIONS FORMED
THROUGH TOUCHPOINTS

• WEBSITE • ADS • EMAIL • CUSTOMER SERVICE

MANAGE YOUR BRAND BY MANAGING YOUR
• TOUCHPOINTS •

Brands are NOT logos, graphics, or slogans. Those are artifacts that can help with familiarity with your brand, but a brand is much deeper. What impression is left on your customers? What are your touchpoints with them?

3 BRANDING ESSENTIALS

① RESONATE WITH CONSUMERS

② DIFFERENTIATE FROM COMPETITORS

③ MOTIVATE EMPLOYEES

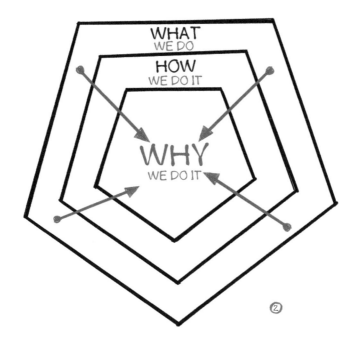

WHAT: WE BRING KIDS HAPPINESS

HOW: BY MAKING TOYS

WHY : BECAUSE CHILDREN ARE OUR FUTURE AND EACH ONE
DESERVES TO SMILE IN A DARKENING WORLD.

We think people care about what we do, or how we do it. Actually, they don't. People care about WHY we do what we do. That is who we are at our core — and that becomes our brand mantra, which acts as guardrails on all decisions we are considering. Ask: "Does this decision align with our core?" If not, don't do it.

BRAND MANTRA
WHAT WE ARE AT OUR CORE

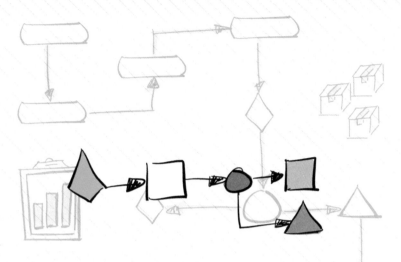

CHAPTER SEVEN

OPERATIONS
MANAGEMENT

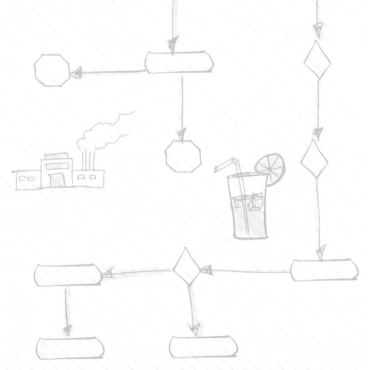

Ops management is broken down into 3 parts. You are designing, managing, and improving a set of activities that creates products and services and delivers them to customers.

DESIGN   MANAGE   IMPROVE ①

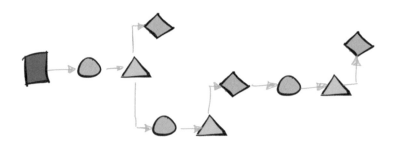

Whenever starting a new position or responsibility, don't feel overwhelmed. Keep calm, and map the process. Look for complexity and simplify.

 PROCESS ANALYSIS

① UNDERSTAND THE CURRENT OPERATION

② UNDERSTAND THE PERFORMANCE

③ UNDERSTAND PERFORMANCE REQUIRED BY CUSTOMERS

PERFORMANCE

CAPACITY

Max output units per unit of time (100 pizzas per hour).

EFFICIENCY

Utilization. You have 100 workers who normally work 8hrs. If in a day there were only 700 hours fully consumed you would be 87.5% efficient.

$$700/(100 \times 8) = 87.5\%$$

KEY TERMS

Lead Time: The time between a request and the delivery of your product to the customer

Throughput: The amount of a product a business can create within a period of time

Cycle Time: The total amount of time from the beginning to the end of the process

Capacity: Maximum output from a process, measured in units per unit of time

Efficiency: A business' performance standard. All processes are leveraging resources in the most optimal way

Bottleneck: A process in a linked chain that is slow, reducing the capacity of the whole

RAW MATERIALS

Is your lemonade stand running efficiently? Let's check out your process and see how it's doing.

UNIT =

THROUGHPUT = 1 UNIT AT 2:50

BOTTLENECK = (2:00)

CAPACITY = 5 UNITS PER 12:10

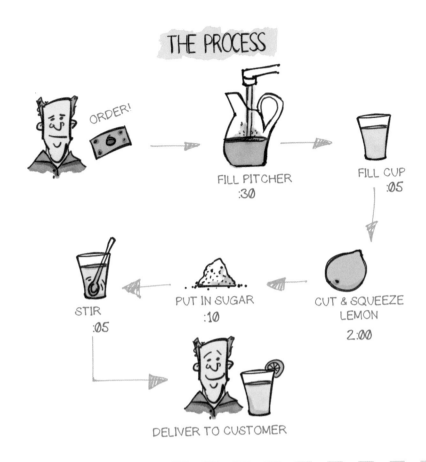

THE PROCESS

ORDER!

FILL PITCHER
:30

FILL CUP
:05

STIR
:05

PUT IN SUGAR
:10

CUT & SQUEEZE
LEMON
2:00

DELIVER TO CUSTOMER

Filling the pitcher happens every 5 cups. Depending on your demand you could constantly be making 5 cups at a time in a batch to meet demand.

Unless you were reducing a cycle time, or removing a bottleneck, each batch would take 12 minutes and 10 seconds. Unless you hire more people, that is your max capacity.

Now, if you usually produce 5 batches an hour (25 cups/hour), you can then figure your capacity utilization. If you only produced 17 cups this hour your capacity utilization would be 17/25 = 68%.

This is a simple example, but the principle can apply anywhere. Keep calm, analyze the process, find ways to improve, and then do it.

CHAPTER EIGHT

STRATEGIC HUMAN RESOURCE MANAGEMENT

Most business problems are symptoms of deeper human or organization issues. Improve at the HR level and you will improve the business overall. People management can be systematized to remove variability and to increase predictability.

A bias-proof way to interview and hire. (I have tried this when hiring people and it works well!)

SYSTEMATIC HRING

1. IDENTIFY PURPOSE FOR HIRE

2. PUT TOGETHER JOB DEFINITION

3. DEFINE TASKS

4. PRIORITIZE TASKS

5. DEFINE NEEDED COMPETENCIES
   Ex. Operations Management

6. ASK BEHAVIORAL QUESTIONS & RATE RESPONSES
   Ex. "TELL US ABOUT A TIME WHEN YOU
   CREATED A NEW OPERATIONAL PROCESS."

	JOHN	SALLY	MIKE
OPERATIONAL PROCESS	5	3	1
LEADERSHIP	2	5	1
PROBLEM SOLVING	2	5	2

WEIGHTED BASED ON PRIORITY

AVG.

7. HIRE & ONBOARD

8. EVALUATE EMPLOYEE

SO MUCH OF THE KNOWLEDGE ECONOMY WORK IS DISCRETIONARY

TO GET STUFF DONE PEOPLE HAVE TO

WANT

TO

So how do you motivate employees? See how you hold up with the Motivating Potential Score. This measures how motivated your current employees are.

MOTIVATING POTENTIAL SCORE
1–7 pts (Max 343)

SEEING IMPROVEMENT

MPS = ((SKILL VARIETY + TASK IDENTITY + TASK SIGNIFICANCE) / 3) x AUTONOMY x FEEDBACK

WELCOME!   GOODBYE

TURN OVER (NO BUENO)

COST: 93–200% ANNUAL SALARY

ANNUALIZED TURNOVER RATE

$$\frac{\text{\# OF EXITS}}{\text{AVG. \# OF EMPLOYEES DURING PERIOD}} \times \frac{12}{\text{MONTHS IN A PERIOD}}$$

HERZBERG'S
MOTIVATION-HYGIENE THEORY ②

MOTIVATION

OPPORTUNITIES FOR ACHIEVEMENT

RECOGNITION

REWARDING WORK, MATCHED TO SKILLS

RESPONSIBILITY

ADVANCEMENT

HYGIENE

POOR, OBSTRUCTIVE POLICIES

INTRUSIVE SUPERVISION

JOB LOSS FEARS

UNMEANINGFUL WORK

TRACK HIGH POTENTIALS
FACILITATE THEIR DEVELOPMENT

PERFORMANCE
MANAGEMENT

 SET PERFORMANCE EXPECTATIONS

 MEASURE RESULTS

 PROVIDE FEEDBACK

 REWARD or CORRECT

PERFORMANCE =

COMPETENCY x MOTIVATION x OPPORTUNITY

- TRAINING   - INCENTIVES   - SUPPORT
                                          - ROLE DEFINITION
                                          - ADDED
                                            RESPONSIBILITY

TEAM SUCCESS LEVERS

- Team skills
- Motivation
- Team size

TEAM PERFORMANCE ③

Context →

- Need for a team
- Type of team needed
- Team culture

Ability to monitor & improve performance

Competencies

Team's ability to solve problems, communicate, make decisions, manage conflict, innovate

---

When meeting any kind of resistance, appeal to the emotions. Logic is like a man riding an elephant (emotion). Guess who decides where to go?

CHAPTER NINE

BUSINESS NEGOTIATIONS

WE NEGOTIATE

30 x / Day

BARGAINER CHARACTERISTICS

NEGOTIATION FRAMEWORK

NEGOTIATION PROCESS

NEGOTIATION OUTCOMES

SITUATIONAL FACTORS

The negotiation framework is simple yet powerful. Apply this framework and get what you want much more often.

BARGAINER CHARACTERISTICS

LISTEN

#1 ON THE LIST

INTERPERSONAL ORIENTATION

Owls are great
negotiators

WILLING TO USE
TEAM ASSISTANCE

- LISTEN
- OBSERVE
- ASK QUESTIONS
  "WHO"

SOCIAL COMPETENCE

Compliments don't cost much,
but they are effective.

What do you want them to think of you?

✓ Fair & honest
✓ Knowledgeable, done homework
✓ Walk away

SOURCES OF INDIVIDUAL
POWER ①

① LEGITIMATE POWER
   - JUDGE
   - POLICE

② REWARD/COERCIVE POWER
   - SCARCE RESOURCES

③ EXPERT POWER
   - SKILLS
   - KNOWLEDGE

④ REFERENT POWER
   - "X SENT ME"
   - DIPLOMATS

⑤ PERSONAL POWER
   - CHARM
   - CHARISMA
   - POLITICIANS

CRITICAL
ATTRIBUTES

- Even temperament
- Discipline
- Excellent listener

LISTEN   TALK

3 ATTRIBUTES OF PERSUASION

1. POWER
- Preparation
- Expert
- Personal

2. CREDIBILITY
- "I don't know"
- "Right" outcome

3. ATTRACTIVENESS
- Message
- Messenger
  - Listens
  - Builds trust
  - Pays attention

Never fall in love
with one

Fall in love with

Power in a negotiation
is in your BATNA

E L O G
S T E R
T E G E
   R O E
   N T M
   A I E
   T A N
   I T T
   V E
   E D

 SITUATIONAL FACTORS

- GOALS (BUYER & SELLER)

- INTERESTS

- SETTING (TIME & PLACE)

NEEDS ALTERNATIVES MATRIX (POWER)

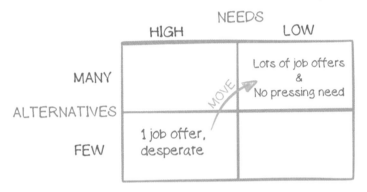

	NEEDS	
	HIGH	LOW
MANY ALTERNATIVES		Lots of job offers & No pressing need
FEW	1 job offer, desperate	

Parties with more alternatives and lower needs have the most power. How can you put yourself in a position of power when negotiating? Also, how can you adapt to a situation where the other party has more power?

 NEGOTIATION PROCESS

CRITICAL

Role-play before the negotiation
(Even if over the phone)
The game changer
Role-play both sides.
Know it better than they.

Pro tip: Write out your opening statement ahead of time.

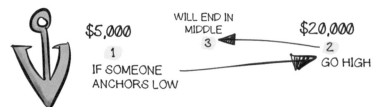

$5,000

1

IF SOMEONE
ANCHORS LOW

WILL END IN
MIDDLE
3

$20,000

2

GO HIGH

"THE EARLIER YOU DISCUSS
MONEY, THE LESS MONEY
YOU WILL GET."

PRINCIPLED NEGOTIATION
②

1 SEPARATE PEOPLE
FROM PROBLEM

2 FOCUS ON INTERESTS
NOT POSITIONS

VS

3 LOOK FOR OPTIONS
FOR MUTUAL GAIN

4 USE FAIR STANDARDS
AND PROCEDURES

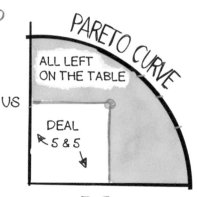

PARETO CURVE

ALL LEFT
ON THE TABLE

US

DEAL
↖ 5 & 5
↘

THEM
Get info to know how to
expand the curve for
both parties

COGNITIVE ANCHORING

Explanation **FIRST** then conclusion

"This pen went to the moon and
back"

"It's only $8,000"

The best negotiators don't
go in linear order

 they
manuver

their

points

on the fly
You have to know them
ahead of time.

(Write them down)

① WHAT IS YOUR GOAL?

Your goal is paramount. Do you want to be right . . . . or do you want to achieve a happy marriage? Sometimes you can't have both.

② WHO ARE YOU NEGOTIATING WITH?

The more you know and understand this person, the better your chances are of a successful negotiated outcome. What are the "pictures in their head"? What keeps them up at night? What are their hopes and dreams?

③

③ WHAT IS YOUR INCREMENTAL PLAN?

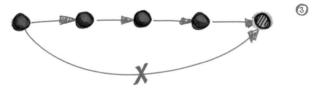

③

Being incremental wins every time vs. trying to get everything right off the bat.

CHAPTER TEN
STRATEGY

THE 5 COMPETITIVE FORCES THAT SHARE STRATEGY ①

These 5 forces can determine the long-term profitability of a company. The higher the threat, the lower the profits. Either build a defense against these forces or find an industry where the forces are weaker.

HIGHER THREAT
=
LOWER PROFITS

DO THINGS
DIFFERENTLY

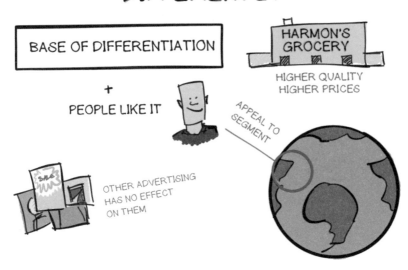

BASE OF DIFFERENTIATION

+

PEOPLE LIKE IT

OTHER ADVERTISING HAS NO EFFECT ON THEM

HARMON'S GROCERY

HIGHER QUALITY
HIGHER PRICES

APPEAL TO SEGMENT

Appeal to a customer segment, find a base of differentiation, and the competition's advertising will have no effect. Be so amazing that customers naturally prefer you.

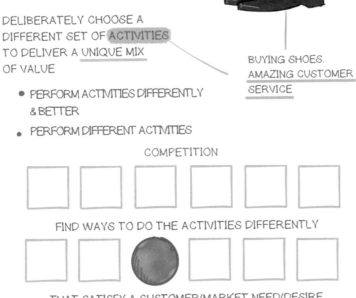

DELIBERATELY CHOOSE A DIFFERENT SET OF ACTIVITIES TO DELIVER A UNIQUE MIX OF VALUE

- PERFORM ACTIVITIES DIFFERENTLY & BETTER
- PERFORM DIFFERENT ACTIVITIES

BUYING SHOES.
AMAZING CUSTOMER SERVICE

COMPETITION

FIND WAYS TO DO THE ACTIVITIES DIFFERENTLY

THAT SATISFY A CUSTOMER/MARKET NEED/DESIRE

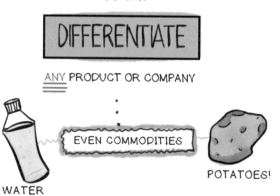

DIFFERENTIATE

ANY PRODUCT OR COMPANY

EVEN COMMODITIES

WATER

POTATOES!

Differentiation just takes creativity. Look around and find some object. If you were selling that object, how would you differentiate it? If someone can do this with commodities, you can too.

BASES OF DIFFERENTIATION

"GREAT DIFFERENTIATORS KNOW WHAT THEIR CUSTOMERS WANT"

FILLS SOME CUSTOMER NEED

• IMAGE	• BEAUTY	• SAFETY	• FURTHER A CAUSE
• HUNGER	• STATUS	• QUALITY	• RELIABILITY
• COMFORT	• STYLE	• SERVICE	• NOSTALGIA
• CLEANLINESS	• TASTE	• ACCURACY	• BELONGING

VS. VS.

MOST PEOPLE CAN'T
TELL THE DIFFERENCE

 —— IF PEOPLE CAN'T TELL
THE DIFFERENCE, HOW
DO THEY DIFFERENTIATE?

HAPPINESS

MARKETING & APPEAL
TO TARGET

HOW COULD YOU COMPETE
AGAINST THEM AS A NEW
COLA?

HINT: NOT TASTE

BASIS OF COMPETITION ISN'T
THE PRODUCT

INDUSTRY STRUCTURE
MATTERS ⟶ PERFECTLY COMPETITIVE?
(ALL 5 FORCES MAXIMIZED)
STAY AWAY

HARLEY

IF YOU WANT TO COMPETE,
YOU HAVE TO UNDERSTAND
WHY PEOPLE ARE
BUYING

MAKING
A BETTER BIKE
WON'T BRING
CUSTOMERS. THEY
ARE BUYING A
LIFESTYLE.

A STRATEGY IS ONLY AS GOOD AS YOUR

IMPLEMENTATION

RECOGNIZE THINGS AS
THEY REALLY ARE
RATHER THAN WHAT THEY
OUGHT TO BE

During the Civil War, the Confederate army at Gettysburg had a better strategy but they didn't recognize and adapt to new circumstances. The result? Well .... you know the rest.

RIP

GETTYSBURG

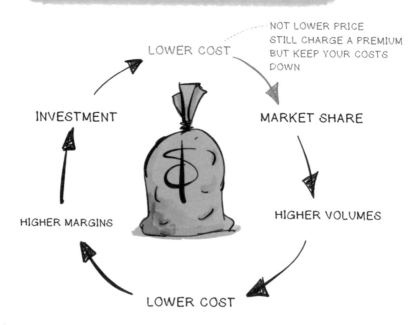

—•• LOW COST STRATEGY •—

LOWER COST

NOT LOWER PRICE
STILL CHARGE A PREMIUM
BUT KEEP YOUR COSTS
DOWN

INVESTMENT

MARKET SHARE

HIGHER MARGINS

HIGHER VOLUMES

LOWER COST

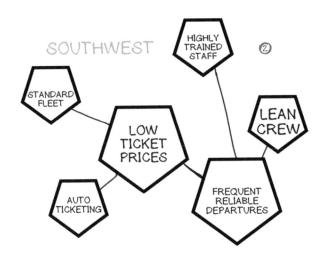

SOUTHWEST

HIGHLY TRAINED STAFF

②

STANDARD FLEET

LEAN CREW

LOW TICKET PRICES

AUTO TICKETING

FREQUENT RELIABLE DEPARTURES

A company creates a strategic advantage when it has various connected activities that support its core differentiating value. Southwest was able to beat other airlines with low ticket prices by using auto ticketing and a standardized fleet along with frequent reliable departures and by using a lean, highly trained staff.

DISNEY

HOW DO YOU MAKE YOUR COMPANY LIKE DISNEY? THAT'S WHAT STRATEGY IS ALL ABOUT.

PRODUCT, MARKETING MESSAGING, POSITIONING, CUSTOMER SERVICE, ETC.

=

OVERALL MAGICAL EXPERIENCE

CUSTOMERS HAVE SUCH PASSION FOR YOU THAT THEY ARE IMPERVIOUS TO THE COMPETITION, MAKING THE COMPETITION IRRELEVANT

COMPETITOR
ANALYSIS ⟶

IT'S A GAME

PLAYERS: YOU & YOUR COMPETITOR
ACTION: ENTER A NEW MARKET
PRODUCT: TRAMPOLINES
PRODUCTION: $75/UNIT
COST

WOULD BUY
200,000 UNITS
@ $250

NEW UNTAPPED
MARKET

35 mil

$35,000,000
-12,000,000
23,000,000

FIXED
COST
$12 mil

FACTORY

⟶ GO FOR IT?!

STOP

"JUMPY"
TRAMPOLINES

WHO ARE THE
POTENTIAL
COMPETITORS?

THE GAME CAN CHANGE

WHAT ARE THEIR FIXED COSTS?
WHAT ARE THEIR PRODUCTION COSTS?
IF THEY ENTER, WILL IT LOWER PRICE?

GATHER DATA
MAKE ASSUMPTIONS

Competitors change the game. You may think all is well with your projections but did you consider what happens when someone else enters? Will it change your sales price and have an impact on your profits? You have to think through the various scenarios before going all in.

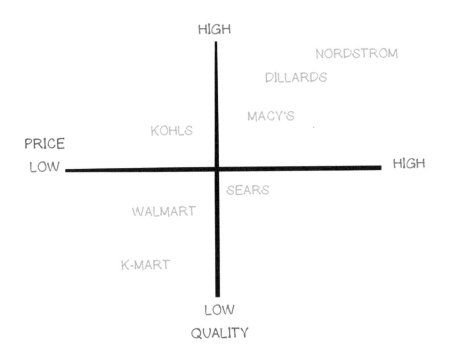

HIGH

NORDSTROM

DILLARDS

MACY'S

KOHLS

PRICE

LOW ———————————————————————— HIGH

SEARS

WALMART

K-MART

LOW

QUALITY

PERSPECTIVE FROM
CUSTOMERS OR COMPETITORS

VRIO FRAMEWORK ③

Is your product, service, company:

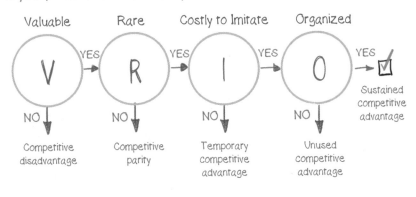

| Valuable | Rare | Costly to Imitate | Organized |

| V | R | I | O |

YES → YES → YES → YES → ☑
Sustained
competitive
advantage

| NO ↓ | NO ↓ | NO ↓ | NO ↓ |

| Competitive disadvantage | Competitive parity | Temporary competitive advantage | Unused competitive advantage |

Running your idea through the VRIO framework can help determine whether or not you will have the chance for a sustained competitive advantage.

RED OCEAN

BLOODY WITH COMPETITION

- COMPETE IN EXISTING MARKET SPACE
- BEAT THE COMPETITION
- EXPLOIT EXISTING DEMAND

BLUE OCEAN

OPEN, UNCONTESTED WATERS

- CREATE UNCONTESTED MARKET SPACE
- MAKE THE COMPETITION IRRELEVANT
- CREATE & CAPTURE NEW DEMAND

 VS.

LUXURY CARS
- EXPENSIVE
- NARROW MARKET
- HIGH PRODUCTION COSTS

MODEL T
- CHEAP
- BROAD MARKET
- LOW PRODUCTION COSTS

There are two types of strategy with regards to competition: Red and Blue oceans. Red oceans are filled with competition. Before the Ford Model T the automobile landscape was expensive. Henry Ford decided to create an uncontested market space with a cheap alternative — and won.

ALLIANCES

NECESSARY TO EXPAND BUSINESS

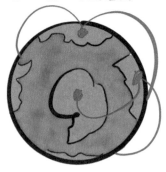

ONLY IF IT PRODUCES COMPLEMENTARY VALUE/RESOURCES

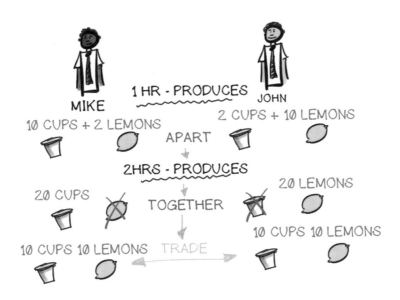

MIKE
1 HR - PRODUCES
JOHN

10 CUPS + 2 LEMONS

2 CUPS + 10 LEMONS

APART

2HRS - PRODUCES

20 CUPS

20 LEMONS

TOGETHER

10 CUPS 10 LEMONS

10 CUPS 10 LEMONS   TRADE

Alliances are critical in expanding your business, but they need to add value that you couldn't get on your own. If Mike can make 10 cups and 2 lemons an hour and John the opposite, you could form an alliance to produce more of both, faster. Make sure you can articulate what specific value they provide and no matter what, make sure you have a legally binding contract set up.

YOU NEED A CONTRACT

WITH ALLIANCES
(EVEN BUSINESS PARTNERSHIPS)

CAN YOU ARTICULATE WHAT VALUE
THEY PROVIDE?

CHAPTER ELEVEN
BUSINESS ETHICS

Business ethics is more than just keeping you out of jail. Living ethically leads to a more fulfilling life, enabling you to leave a legacy you can be proud of.

Disclosure Test

When in doubt ask yourself, "Would I be okay if this decision ended up on the 5:00 news?" If not, then don't do it.

EMOTION

CAUSES SHORT-TERM THINKING

Remember who you want to be

A critical element is moving from short-term thinking to long-term thinking. Most ethical issues arise from emotion, which causes us to think in the short term. All you need to do is to stop and to remember your goals of who you want to be. Will this decision reinforce or take away from that image?

DECISION PROCESS

As emotions are high when ethics are at stake, use this simple process to help guide you in making ethical decisions.

1 - Stop & Think

Don't react. First, just stop and think.

2 - Gather facts

Now you can gather all the facts and information. Is what you are deciding on critical? Can it wait? Who is involved? What's at stake?

3 - Brainstorm solutions

Your decision is only as good as your best alternative. Take time to brainstorm as many solutions as possible.

4 - Decide

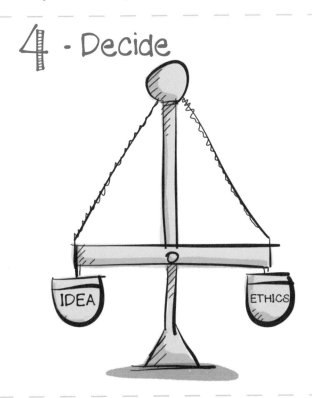

Now it's time to weigh your decision against whether or not it is ethical. It helps to run things by others to make sure your judgment isn't clouded.

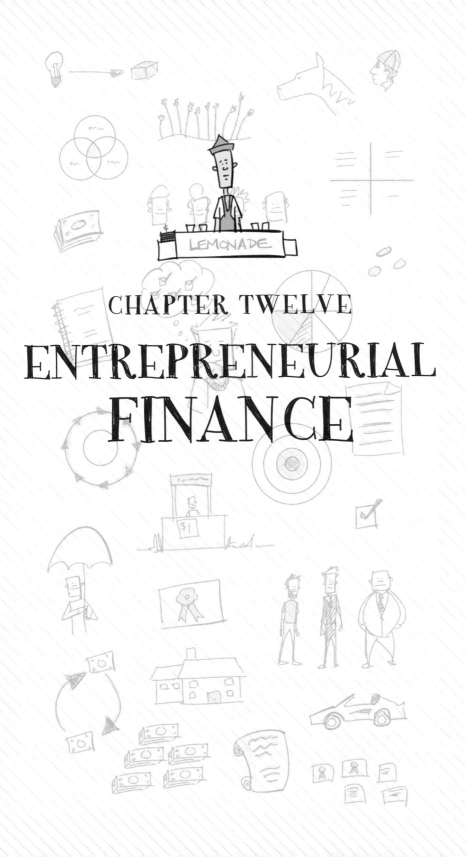

CHAPTER TWELVE

ENTREPRENEURIAL FINANCE

Entrepreneurial Finance is all about creating value as quickly as possible through a series of strategic activities.

Entrepreneurial Finance Process

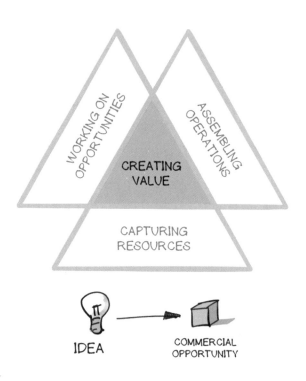

WORKING ON OPPORTUNITIES

ASSEMBLING OPERATIONS

CREATING VALUE

CAPTURING RESOURCES

IDEA ⟶ COMMERCIAL OPPORTUNITY

What is your END GAME?

THE HARVEST

The goal is always the harvest and how to get there as quickly as possible.

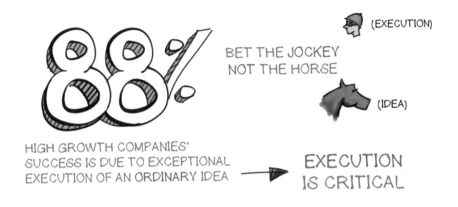

88%

BET THE JOCKEY
NOT THE HORSE

(EXECUTION)

(IDEA)

HIGH GROWTH COMPANIES'
SUCCESS IS DUE TO EXCEPTIONAL
EXECUTION OF AN ORDINARY IDEA ➡️

EXECUTION
IS CRITICAL

There are tons of opportunities out there. It is just up to you to find them. The following are some opportunity sources where you should always keep a finger on the pulse.

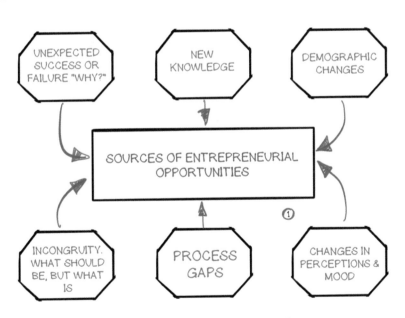

UNEXPECTED SUCCESS OR FAILURE "WHY?"

NEW KNOWLEDGE

DEMOGRAPHIC CHANGES

SOURCES OF ENTREPRENEURIAL OPPORTUNITIES

①

INCONGRUITY. WHAT SHOULD BE, BUT WHAT IS

PROCESS GAPS

CHANGES IN PERCEPTIONS & MOOD

Create an industry that solves the problems
that arise from these factors

Before diving head first into your idea, make sure it is feasible. You will be spending a lot of time on it so you'd better do some validation first. Look at your internal and external forces, and then map it out with a SWOT analysis.

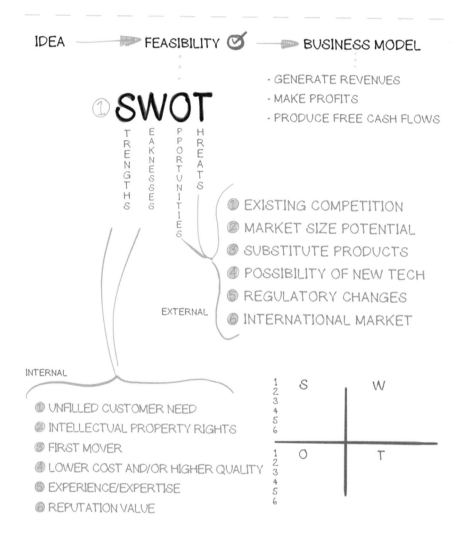

IDEA ⟶ FEASIBILITY ☑ ⟶ BUSINESS MODEL

① SWOT

- GENERATE REVENUES
- MAKE PROFITS
- PRODUCE FREE CASH FLOWS

S T R E N G T H S | W E A K N E S S E S | O P P O R T U N I T I E S | H R E A T S

EXTERNAL

① EXISTING COMPETITION
② MARKET SIZE POTENTIAL
③ SUBSTITUTE PRODUCTS
④ POSSIBILITY OF NEW TECH
⑤ REGULATORY CHANGES
⑥ INTERNATIONAL MARKET

INTERNAL

① UNFILLED CUSTOMER NEED
② INTELLECTUAL PROPERTY RIGHTS
③ FIRST MOVER
④ LOWER COST AND/OR HIGHER QUALITY
⑤ EXPERIENCE/EXPERTISE
⑥ REPUTATION VALUE

1 2 3 4 5 6   S   W

1 2 3 4 5 6   O   T

When looking at any new venture it is helpful to put it through a good screening. Two ways of doing this are through both a quantitative and a qualitative screen. The higher the score, the more appealing to investors.

QUANTITATIVE SCREENING

POTENTIAL ATTRACTIVENESS

	HIGH 3	MEDIUM 2	LOW 1
MARKET SIZE			
PROFITABILITY			
SPEED OF HARVEST			
TEAM CAPABILITY			
VIABILITY			

(Add up the points and divide by 5. The final score will come in between 3 and 1. The closer to 3 the better.)

Quantitative and qualitative screening of a new venture removes emotion and provides the data you need to make a wise decision. First do a quantitative screening and see how close to a score of 3 you get. Then take a look at the management team and ask questions to flesh out their vision, knowledge, and plans for the future.

QUALITATIVE SCREENING
INTERVIEW MANAGEMENT TEAM

FOUNDER   MARKETING   OPS   FINANCE

PRODUCTION

CUSTOMER
KNOWLEDGE

BIG PICTURE

FINANCIAL
PREDICTIONS

⬆ HIGH GROWTH BEST PRACTICES ⬆

MARKETING PRACTICES

- DEVELOP THE BEST PRODUCT OR SERVICE
- HIGH QUALITY PRODUCT OR SERVICE
- PRODUCT COMMANDS HIGHER PRICES
- EFFICIENT DISTRIBUTION & SUPERIOR SUPPORT

FINANCIAL PRACTICES

- PREP DETAILED MONTHLY FINANCIAL PLANS & ANNUAL FINANCIAL PLAN FOR THE NEXT 5 YEARS
- EFFECTIVELY MANAGE THE FIRM'S ASSETS, FINANCIAL RESOURCES, & OPERATING PERFORMANCE

MANAGEMENT PRACTICES

- ASSEMBLE MANAGEMENT TEAM BALANCED IN BOTH FUNCTIONAL AREAS & INDUSTRY KNOWLEDGE
- COLLABORATIVE DECISION MAKING

THESE ARE FOR YOU (MAKES YOU THINK OF ALL AREAS)

BUSINESS PLAN

VENTURE LIFE CYCLE

- DEVELOPMENT   SEED FINANCING

- STARTUP   STARTUP FINANCING

- GROWTH   FIRST-ROUND

- EXPANSION   SECOND-ROUND
                   MEZZANINE
                   LIQUIDITY STAGE

- MATURITY   OBTAINING BANK LOANS
   (POTENTIAL EXIT)   ISSUING BONDS
                   ISSUING STOCK

Any new venture goes through 5 stages that correlate with fundraising. This starts with the initial development and seed financing to get you going, all the way to early maturity.

VENTURE CAPITAL

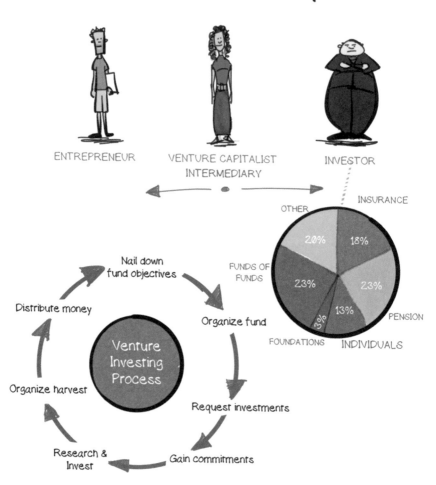

ENTREPRENEUR

VENTURE CAPITALIST
INTERMEDIARY

INVESTOR

INSURANCE

OTHER

FUNDS OF
FUNDS

20%

18%

23%

23%

13%

3%

PENSION

FOUNDATIONS

INDIVIDUALS

Venture Investing Process

Nail down fund objectives

Organize fund

Request investments

Gain commitments

Research & Invest

Organize harvest

Distribute money

TYPICAL COMPENSATION

20 - 2

20% PROFITS
AKA: CARRIED
INTEREST

2% ANNUAL
PAYBACK

DIVERSITY OF OPINION THE VENTURE
INVESTING COMMUNITY CRITICAL TO SUCCESS

MOST VCS SPEND
ON THE INITIAL

 6

MINUTES
SCREENING

VCS CARE MOST ABOUT:
MANAGEMENT TEAM & MARKET

 FINANCING

BEST TO FINANCE
THROUGH SELLING
SHARES
(ALTHOUGH YOU GIVE
UP OWNERSHIP)

TARGET

3x RETURN
OR
6x RETURN

WRITTEN
AGREEMENT

VC VALUATION

When working with VCs they are looking for a 3x-6x return and will need a written agreement. Always remember that in the world of private equity, your reputation means everything. Be true to your word and deliver on what you promise..

PRIVATE **E**QUITY

IT'S ALL ABOUT
REPUTATION

Business Entities

When starting a business it is important to know the positives and negatives of the various business entities before you choose one. Each one can have important implications regarding your exposure to liability and taxes. Here they are below:

Sole proprietorship

Simple and the most common among the entities. It is unincorporated and doesn't make any distinction between the owner and the business. But with the simplicity comes some risk. Without a distinction between the owner and the business, your personal assets are at risk if someone decides to sue you.

LLC

LLC stands for Limited Liability Corporation. This is usually a better choice over a sole proprietorship as it creates a legal buffer between the owner and the business. This entity combines the characteristics of a sole proprietorship and a corporation.

S Corp

More complicated with added rules and regulations. With that said, this might be preferable if you are looking for outside financing or issuing stock. Having the flexibility to issue stock is always nice as it can incentivize partnerships or provide additional help with the business.

C Corp

C Corps are like S Corps, but are taxed twice (net income of the corporation and also when shareholders' profits are distributed). C Corps can have unlimited shareholders whereas S Corps can only have a max of 100 and they must be U.S. citizens.

5C'S OF CREDIT

The 5 C's of credit are what lenders use when evaluating potential borrowers.

① CHARACTER

CREDIT HISTORY & REPUTATION

CHARACTER can also be referred to as credit history. This is the info on the credit reports of the borrower. These reports show how much you have borrowed over time and whether or not you have repaid your loans on time.

② CAPACITY

ABILITY TO REPAY

CAPACITY is your ability to repay the loan. This is a comparison of your current income against your recurring debts. Lenders are also looking at how long you have been at your current job when making this assessment.

③ CAPITAL

CONTRIBUTION OF THE BORROWER

CAPITAL is what you as a borrower are already putting towards the investment. This helps lenders feel more secure that you won't default on your loan.

④ COLLATERAL

ASSETS PUT UP BY THE BORROWER

COLLATERAL is the assets you put up as security in the event that the loan defaults. This gives the lender options to liquidate your assets in order to get their money back.

⑤ CONDITIONS

HOW THE BORROWER WILL USE IT

CONDITIONS include the amount borrowed, the interest rate, and how the borrower plans to use the money. The clearer and more focused the purpose, the greater the chances of getting the loan approved.

CHAPTER THIRTEEN

JUDGMENT AND DECISION MAKING

Decisions affect your life and happen on a daily basis. Learn how to make the best ones possible in order to achieve stellar results.

BE PROACTIVE

 - PROBLEM

OUR SUCCESS DEPENDS ON THE DECISIONS WE MAKE

 - OBJECTIVES

 - ALTERNATIVES

EVEN THE MOST COMPLEX DECISIONS CAN BE MADE WITH THIS PROCESS

 - CONSEQUENCES

 - TRADE OFFS ①

This model works wonders. It is dead simple but can speed up the decision-making process significantly and help you land in the right spot.

 **Pr** WORK ON THE **RIGHT** DECISION PROBLEM

This is the most important step. Make sure you put together a well-posed decision problem and that it is the RIGHT problem to solve. Example: "Which gym should I join?" vs. "How might I improve my health?"

  LIST ALL YOUR OBJECTIVES

One by one, go through your objectives. Ask the question, what do we want from this? Then ask, why? You might be surprised at what you discover.

 BRAINSTORM YOUR ALTERNATIVES

This part is so important. You will only make a decision as good as your best alternative. Take time to come up with a number of alternatives.

OBJECTIVES | ALTERNATIVES

THEN
RANK 3–1
(H) (L)

Consequences. On a spreadsheet, map out your objectives in the column on the left with all your alternatives along the top and then weight them. Then go through each alternative and score it 1–3 based on how well it meets each objective. This will give you a pretty good indicator which direction to go.

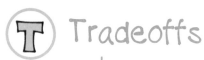

T Tradeoffs

	Car 1	Car 2	Car 3
Comfort	3	3	2
Roominess	2	3	2
Attractiveness	2	3	3
Low miles	1	1	3
Condition	3	1	3
Price	2	1	3

You should have a pretty good idea by now which direction to go, but it is good to look at the tradeoffs you will need to make for any alternatives that are close.

PRACTICE MAKES PERMANENT

NEW GOLF GRIP. PRACTICE
SWINGING 100 TIMES
FEELS WEIRD AT FIRST,
THEN BECOMES NATURAL

This is a great model to help you make better decisions but it isn't natural. With focused practice it will become second nature to you. Practice, practice, practice.

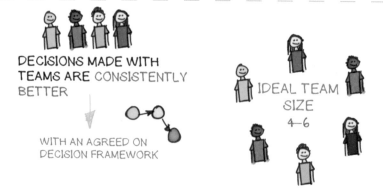

DECISIONS MADE WITH
TEAMS ARE CONSISTENTLY
BETTER

WITH AN AGREED ON
DECISION FRAMEWORK

IDEAL TEAM
SIZE
4–6

How often have you been in a situation where people rushed to solve a problem, only to find out it was the wrong one? This is a common decision trap that happens too often. Below are a few common traps we all fall into. Beware.

TRAPS

- ABSENCE OF A SIMPLE, POWERFUL, SHARED JUDGMENT PROCESS MODEL

- THE RUSH TO SOLVE
  WE END UP SOLVING THE **WRONG** PROBLEM

- SPECIFY, ARTICULATE, AND EVALUATE THE DECISION TRIGGER
  - THING THAT MAKES YOU AWARE OF THE PROBLEM
  TIP: COULD BE AN ALTERNATIVE MASQUERADING AS A PROBLEM

"IS THIS REALLY A PROBLEM OR AN ALTERNATIVE?"
JOB RECRUITER CALLS. TAKE JOB?
NOT A PROBLEM!

THE MAGIC QUESTION

SAVE X FOR RETIREMENT
WHY?   MEANS TO
.   AN END
.
SPEND TIME WITH FAMILY
(TRUE OBJECTIVE)

WHY?

GOOD TEST TO VALIDATE OBJECTIVES

We all look at the world through different perspectives (frames). The more you can see the world from others' perspectives, the better off you will be.

SEE A SITUATION FROM MULTIPLE PERSPECTIVES

IDENTIFY: YOUR FRAME. OTHERS' FRAMES.

LOOK AT PROBLEMS FROM MANY FRAMES & PULL OUT THE BEST IDEAS

THIS IS HARD. COGNITIVE DISSONANCE. GIVE YOURSELF PERMISSION TO DISAGREE AFTER. (WAR ON DRUGS)

This isn't easy but it can be done with some practice. Take a hard topic that you don't agree with and give yourself permission to see it from an opposing perspective. The more angles you can see it from, the more informed you will be to make a better decision.

There are two types of thinking: system 1 and system 2. Our minds generally default to system 1 because it is faster and simpler. This can be dangerous if we always default to system 1 for tough decisions. The two best ways to battle this are to be aware of the various biases and to follow a structured problem-solving method.

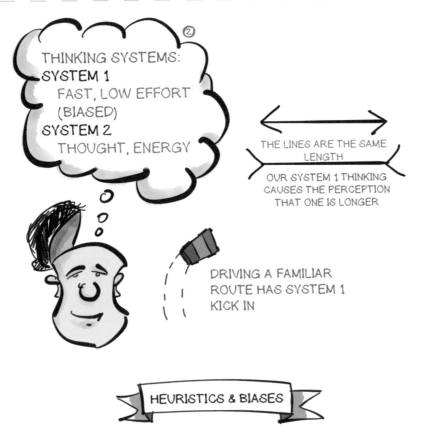

THINKING SYSTEMS:
SYSTEM 1
    FAST, LOW EFFORT
    (BIASED)
SYSTEM 2
    THOUGHT, ENERGY

THE LINES ARE THE SAME LENGTH

OUR SYSTEM 1 THINKING CAUSES THE PERCEPTION THAT ONE IS LONGER

DRIVING A FAMILIAR ROUTE HAS SYSTEM 1 KICK IN

HEURISTICS & BIASES

① AVAILABILITY HEURISTIC

② REPRESENTATIVENESS HEURISTIC

③ PROSPECT THEORY

④ ANCHORING & INSUFFICIENT ADJUSTMENT

⑤ OVERCONFIDENCE

⑥ MOTIVATED REASONING

AVAILABILITY HEURISTIC ③
PEOPLE BASE PREDICTIONS ON HOW EASILY AN EXAMPLE CAN BE BROUGHT TO MIND

PRIMACY

MOST WEIGHT ON
INITIAL INFO

RECENCY

MOST WEIGHT ON MOST
RECENT INFO

SURROGATION

MEASURE BECOMES THE
STRATEGY

REPRESENTATIVENESS HEURISTIC ④
PEOPLE JUDGE THE LIKELIHOOD OF AN EVENT'S OCCURANCE BY THE DEGREE IT REPRESENTS THE DATA

BASE RATE NEGLECT

PEOPLE ASSESS
PROBABILITY OF AN
EVENT WITHOUT
TAKING ACCOUNT OF
THE BASE RATE
PROBABILITY

GAMBLER'S FALLACY

WITH 3 HEADS IN
A ROW, WE EXPECT
IT TO EVEN OUT

HOT HAND FALLACY

WE THINK RANDOM
SHOULD BE RANDOM.
WHEN IT'S NOT, WE
THINK THE HAND IS
HOT

ILLUSORY AND INVISIBLE CORRELATIONS

1, 19, 152, 99, 107

WE SEE CORRELATIONS
WHEN THEY AREN'T
THERE OR MISS THEM
WHEN THEY ARE

PROSPECT THEORY ⑤
PEOPLE ARE LOSS AVERSE. THEY PREFER AVOIDING LOSS TO ACQUIRING GAINS, LEADING TO RISK SEEKING IN LOSS DOMAIN & RISK AVERSE IN THE GAIN DOMAIN

LOSS AVERSION

PREFER ALLEVIATING
RISK OF LOSS OVER
SEEKING GAIN

DISPOSITION EFFECT

HOLD LOSING STOCKS
LONGER THAN WINNING
STOCKS

FRAMING EFFECTS

THE WAY THE
PROBLEM IS FRAMED
DETERMINES OUTCOME

FAIRNESS CONCERNS

PEOPLE MAKE ECONOMICALLY
IRRATIONAL DECISIONS
TO AVOID UNFAIRNESS

ANCHORING & INSUFFICIENT ADJUSTMENT

PEOPLE TEND TO RELY TOO HEAVILY ON A NUMBER "ANCHOR" (EVEN A RANDOM ONE) WHEN MAKING DECISIONS

CURSE OF KNOWLEDGE

PEOPLE HAVE A HARD TIME BEHAVING AS THEY DID BEFORE OBTAINING INFO

HINDSIGHT BIAS

PEOPLE AREN'T GOOD AT RECALLING THE WAY AN UNCERTAIN SITUATION APPEARED BEFORE OUTCOME

OVERCONFIDENCE

PEOPLE TEND TO BE EXCESSIVELY CONFIDENT IN THEIR PREDICTIONS

"I AM 99% SURE!"

"THEY COULDN'T HIT AN ELEPHANT AT THIS DIST..." - GEN. JOHN B. SEDGWICK

MOTIVATED REASONING

PEOPLE TEND TO EVALUATE EVIDENCE IN WAYS CONSISTENT WITH THEIR PREFERENCES

WISHFUL THINKING

PEOPLE FORM BELIEFS BASED ON WHAT THEY'D LIKE RATHER THAN LOOKING AT DATA

CONFIRMATION BIAS

PEOPLE SEEK CONFIRMING EVIDENCE TO THEIR HYPOTHESIS & PUT MORE WEIGHT ON IT THAN DISCONFIRMING EVIDENCE

INFORMATION PURSUIT BIAS

PURSUING INFO LEADS TO US PUTTING MORE WEIGHT ON IT

SUNK COST FALLACY

THE HIGHER THE SUNK COSTS, THE MORE LIKELY PEOPLE STAY THE COURSE

GROUPS

USUALLY MAKE BETTER JUDGMENTS

① **PREPARATION**
INDIVIDUALS GENERATE IDEAS AHEAD OF TIME

② **DISCUSSION**

 FIRST ROUND
INDIVIDUALS SHARE IDEAS WITHOUT CRITIQUE OR DEBATE

SECOND ROUND
SHARE IDEAS SPARKED BY FIRST ROUND

FINAL ROUND
OPEN DISCUSSION TO RANK IDEAS

CHAPTER FOURTEEN

THE GENERAL MANAGER'S ROLE

General management is all about solving problems and resolving issues — all being accomplished with only limited knowledge. In order for you to help get problems solved, you need to help others frame the problem correctly and to help guide them to the solution.

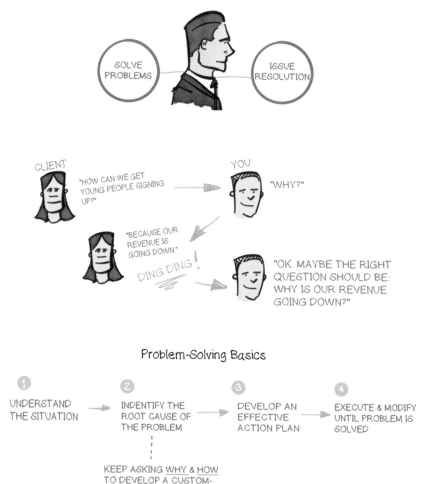

Problem-Solving Basics

① UNDERSTAND THE SITUATION	② INDENTIFY THE ROOT CAUSE OF THE PROBLEM	③ DEVELOP AN EFFECTIVE ACTION PLAN	④ EXECUTE & MODIFY UNTIL PROBLEM IS SOLVED

KEEP ASKING <u>WHY & HOW</u> TO DEVELOP A CUSTOM-MADE ACTION PLAN

Structuring the problem begins by first coming up with a SMART problem definition. Then from there creating an issue tree with all the possible answers to the question.

STRUCTURING THE PROBLEM

"MY GREATEST STRENGTH AS A CONSULTANT IS TO BE IGNORANT AND ASK A FEW QUESTIONS."
—PETER DRUCKER

LEARN TO
ASK GREAT
QUESTIONS

↓

FUNDAMENTAL
PROBLEM

SMART PROBLEM DEFINITION ①

P E C I F I C	E A S U R A B L E	T T A I N A B L T E	E L E V A N T B L E	I M E B O U N D

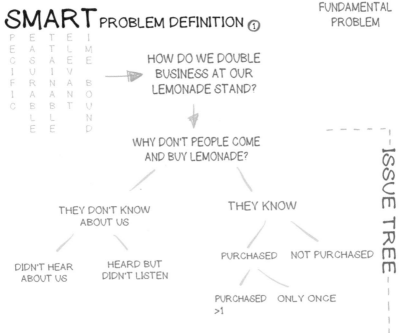

HOW DO WE DOUBLE
BUSINESS AT OUR
LEMONADE STAND?

↓

WHY DON'T PEOPLE COME
AND BUY LEMONADE?

THEY DON'T KNOW
ABOUT US

THEY KNOW

DIDN'T HEAR
ABOUT US

HEARD BUT
DIDN'T LISTEN

PURCHASED   NOT PURCHASED

PURCHASED   ONLY ONCE
>1

ISSUE TREE

Once you have created your issue tree, start testing assumptions, gather data, and cut off branches that don't apply anymore. This helps you get to the root cause and start getting to real solutions.

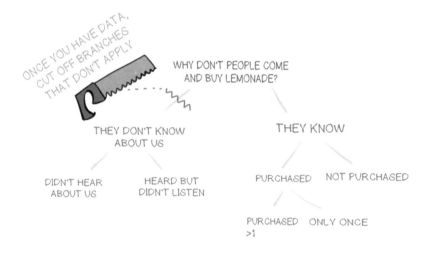

It is important to have your goal that you are solving the problem with front and center. Focus on a goal that has the highest benefit with the lowest cost.

As a consultant you need to provide good recommendations. Below is a basic flow when making recommendations to clients.

GOOD RECOMMENDATIONS

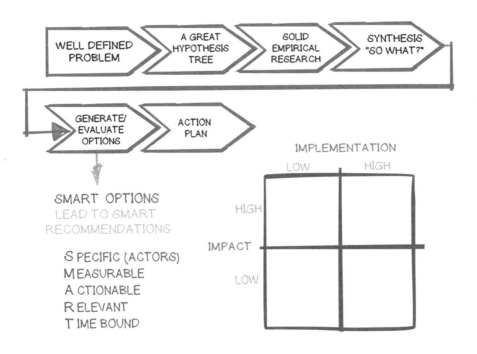

WELL DEFINED PROBLEM → A GREAT HYPOTHESIS TREE → SOLID EMPIRICAL RESEARCH → SYNTHESIS "SO WHAT?"

GENERATE/ EVALUATE OPTIONS → ACTION PLAN

SMART OPTIONS
LEAD TO SMART
RECOMMENDATIONS

S PECIFIC (ACTORS)
M EASURABLE
A CTIONABLE
R ELEVANT
T IME BOUND

IMPLEMENTATION
LOW   HIGH

IMPACT

HIGH

LOW

WHY LEARN ABOUT CHANGE?

GREAT SOLUTIONS CAN FAIL
IF THE ORG ISN'T READY

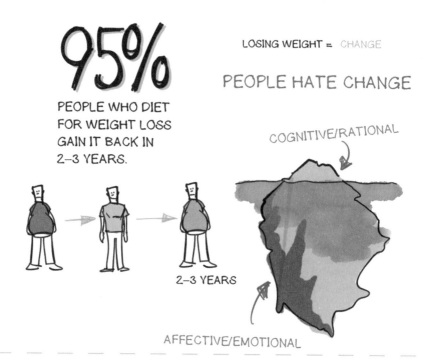

95%

PEOPLE WHO DIET
FOR WEIGHT LOSS
GAIN IT BACK IN
2–3 YEARS.

LOSING WEIGHT = CHANGE

PEOPLE HATE CHANGE

COGNITIVE/RATIONAL

2–3 YEARS

AFFECTIVE/EMOTIONAL

Change is emotional. Find ways to nudge change in the right direction. For example, rather than having you cut back on your food, just start using smaller plates.

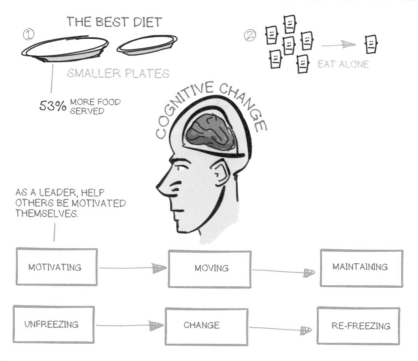

THE BEST DIET

① SMALLER PLATES

53% MORE FOOD SERVED

② EAT ALONE

COGNITIVE CHANGE

AS A LEADER, HELP
OTHERS BE MOTIVATED
THEMSELVES.

MOTIVATING	MOVING	MAINTAINING

UNFREEZING	CHANGE	RE-FREEZING

In order to motivate people to change, you must help them to see and feel the importance of the change.

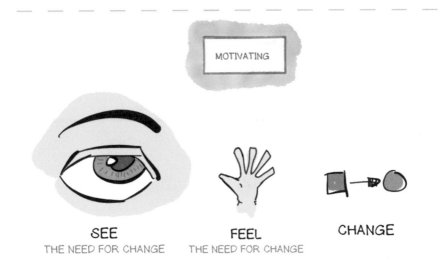

SEE
THE NEED FOR CHANGE

FEEL
THE NEED FOR CHANGE

CHANGE

Change follows an unfreezing of how things have always been, opening up the opportunity for change. Change requires ending the past, leading to a period in a neutral zone, and then settling in the new beginning.

| UNFREEZING | CHANGE | RE-FREEZING |

| ENDING | NEUTRAL ZONE | NEW BEGINNING |

- DISENGAGEMENT
- DISMANTLING
- DISIDENTIFICATION
- DISENCHANTMENT
- DISORIENTED

(TAKEN OUT THE ANCHOR)

- ANXIETY UP, MOTIVATION DOWN
- OLD WEAKNESSES RE-EMERGE
- CONFUSION/ CREATIVITY

- SETTLING IN
- "I'VE ARRIVED"
- SENSE OF SECURITY
- ABILITY TO MOVE FORWARD

IF YOU CAN'T END YOU CAN'T HAVE A NEW BEGINNING

YOU HAVE TO END BEFORE YOU CAN BEGIN. IT TAKES WORK

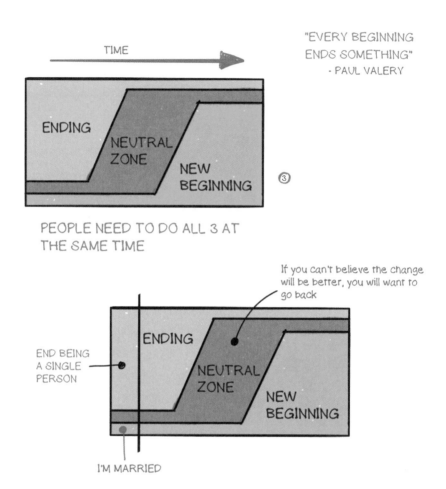

TIME

"EVERY BEGINNING
ENDS SOMETHING"
- PAUL VALERY

ENDING

NEUTRAL ZONE

NEW BEGINNING

③

PEOPLE NEED TO DO ALL 3 AT
THE SAME TIME

If you can't believe the change
will be better, you will want to
go back

END BEING
A SINGLE
PERSON

ENDING

NEUTRAL
ZONE

NEW
BEGINNING

I'M MARRIED

A good example of this is when someone gets married. Exchanging marital vows kicks off the new beginning and requires that the couple end the past of being single and what they were comfortable with in that previous life. This causes them to be in the neutral zone for a time. Believing that the future will be better will enable them to embrace the new beginning, relinquishing the past, and truly changing.

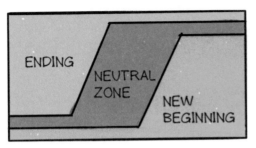

IT IS BETTER TO GO THROUGH
THIS PROCESS THAN DENY IT.
OTHERWISE THE CONSEQUENCES
WILL BE CATASTROPHIC.

CHANGE IS A   HOWEVER   TRANSITION
CUTOFF   ISN'T AS CUT
                          & DRIED

HOW TO GET PEOPLE THROUGH THE CHANGE

① SELL THE PROBLEM, NOT THE SOLUTION
    (EMOTIONALLY)   (COGNITIVELY)

                    REMEMBER, THE ELEPHANT IS
                    MORE POWERFUL.

② IDENTIFY WHO WILL BE LOSING WHAT
    ALLOWS YOU TO PREPARE & EMPATHIZE

③ ACCEPT THE REALITY OF SUBJECTIVE LOSSES
    THE PAIN CAN BE DEEPER THAN YOU REALIZE

④ TREAT THE PAST WITH RESPECT

⑤ BREAKING WITH THE PAST ENSURES CONTINUITY
    OF WHAT REALLY MATTERS

PURPOSE: WHY ARE WE MOVING?

 PICTURE: WHAT WILL IT LOOK LIKE?

 PLAN: HOW WILL WE GET THERE?

 PART: WHERE DO I FIT?

When introducing people to the process of change, help them understand the purpose, picture, plan, and their part. Be patient and remember that although the plans may make sense to you, they may not be there yet or have all the information.

WHERE EVERYONE ELSE IS

YOU ARE HERE AND THINK EVERYONE ELSE IS AS WELL

CAUTION

① REMEMBER THE MARATHON EFFECT ③

YOU MAY HAVE ALREADY CHANGED BUT OTHERS HAVEN'T

② MEASURE TWICE, CUT ONCE

PLAN & PREPARE. IT IS WORTH THE TIME

FIRST TASK OF

CHANGE MANAGEMENT: HELP PEOPLE UNDERSTAND THE DESIRED CHANGE & MAKE IT HAPPEN

↑

WHEN DOING THIS

DON'T FORGET THIS

↓

FIRST TASK OF

TRANSITION MANAGEMENT: CONVINCE PEOPLE TO LEAVE HOME

LOW-COST STRATEGY

FIND POCKETS OF SUPPORT
PROCEED INFORMALLY/SMALL
AT FIRST. BUILD MOMENTUM
AND THEN PROCEED FORMALLY

Large organizational change needs to be strategic, calculated, and precise. It can't be a shotgun model; it has to be more like precise rifle shots.

SHOTGUN VS. RIFLE SHOTS
BUILD THE LOVE GROUP

Warning: Gross. Picture this. You are at dinner with your family and there is a dead dog on the center of the table, but no one talks about it. That is a dysfunctional family. Do you have a dysfunctional organization? What isn't being talked about?

Remember, this needs to be precise. Sharpshooter precise. Ready, aim, fire. Timing, sequencing, and credibility are everything. Plan out your communication strategy and get the right people on board.

MAKING CHANGE IN A LARGE ORG

A change management strategy works by influencing the right people in the org.

CEO

INFLUENCING AT THE TOP DOESN'T TRICKLE DOWN

VP

VP

DIRECTORS

DIRECTORS

WORKERS

DO 1:15 INDIVIDUALLY

CEO

INFORMAL COMMUNICATION

TOP DOWN DOESN'T WORK

DO 1:15 EARLY
YOU ARE SELLING
CHANGE

IT IS NOT "MY PROJECT"

RAISE THE WHOLE ORG

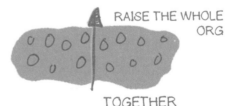

TOGETHER

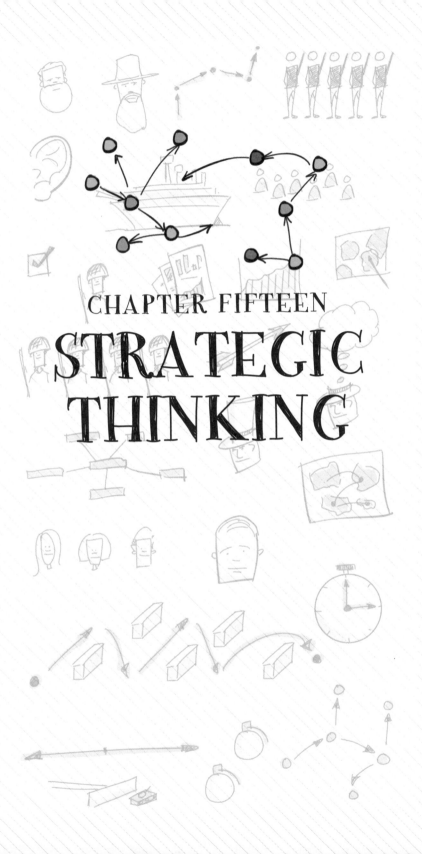

CHAPTER FIFTEEN
STRATEGIC THINKING

By taking a look at history's leaders, we can learn from their successes as well as their failures.

General Lee's men didn't know why he gave certain instructions or why he failed to communicate his thoughts. As a leader, it is easy to have the vision in our minds but if we don't communicate it effectively we will lose the war.

HE DIDN'T LISTEN TO
HIS TRUSTED GENERAL

WHERE IS YOUR
SUCCESS COMING
FROM?

DEFENSIVE STRATEGY
OR
MORALE OF MEN?

You
NEED
TO
ADAPT
TO
CHANGING CIRCUMSTANCES
OR CHANGE THE ENVIRONMENT
SO THE STRATEGY WILL WORK

LEE PUT TOO MUCH
EMPHASIS ON MORALE

GREAT LEADERS
LISTEN

FOR SUCCESS YOU NEED
PEOPLE WHO ARE
COMMITTED & ENGAGED

At a critical time General Lee didn't listen to his generals and was unable to adapt to the changing circumstances around him. Frequently taking inventory of the situation around you and adapting will help you stay on top.

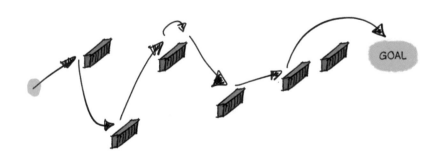

CHURCHILL

Winston Churchill was a leader who was strategic in all he did, including his career, as he intentionally took specific positions to increase his influence.

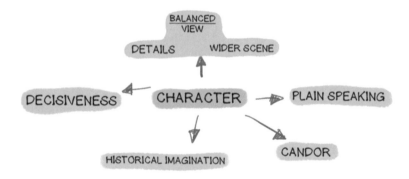

BALANCED
VIEW

DETAILS   WIDER SCENE

DECISIVENESS   CHARACTER   → PLAIN SPEAKING

HISTORICAL IMAGINATION   CANDOR

Churchill valued these character traits as a leader and they served him well in his leadership capacity.

"Success is going from failure to failure without loss of enthusiasm." — Churchill

1
Make key strategic decisions FIRST

2
Choose top leadership

3
Give clear direction, then clear the way for them to act effectively

 PONDER

THEN

 ACT DECISIVELY

RESPONSIBILITY
NEEDS EQUAL
AUTHORITY

For individuals to be successful when given a responsibility, they need to be given equal authority in order to carry out their duties; otherwise it will only lead to failure. Churchill felt that the further back you could look in history, the further ahead you could see.

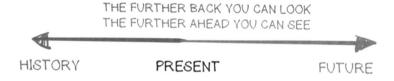

THE FURTHER BACK YOU CAN LOOK
THE FURTHER AHEAD YOU CAN SEE

HISTORY   PRESENT   FUTURE

COLLECTIVE DECISION-MAKING

LEADS TO TEMPORIZING

Counseling together is different than collective decision making. One is about gathering the best insights to help inform a decision; the other only leads to "temporizing" (or meeting in the middle), which is ineffective. Strong leadership listens but also knows when to make a decision.

THE BATTLE OF THE BULGE

  VS.

EISENHOWER	HITLER
• ADAPTED & TRUSTED MILITARY	• ORDER TO NOT DEVIATE
• LISTENED TO STAFF	• DID NOT LISTEN TO STAFF
• LED THROUGH INSPIRING	• LED THROUGH FEAR
• CALM, REASONED, UNPANICKED	• REACTIVE
• WAITED FOR AGREEMENT	• DICTATED
• INTEGRATED STAFF	• CLOSE TO THE VEST
• OPTIMISTIC & BUILT MORALE	• STOIC & INSTILLED FEAR

The Americans rocked the Nazis at the Battle of the Bulge due in large part to Eisenhower's leadership. He led in almost opposite manner and approach to Hitler, and it served Eisenhower well.

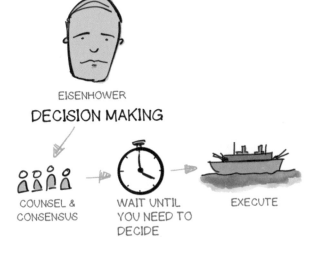

EISENHOWER
DECISION MAKING

COUNSEL & CONSENSUS → WAIT UNTIL YOU NEED TO DECIDE → EXECUTE

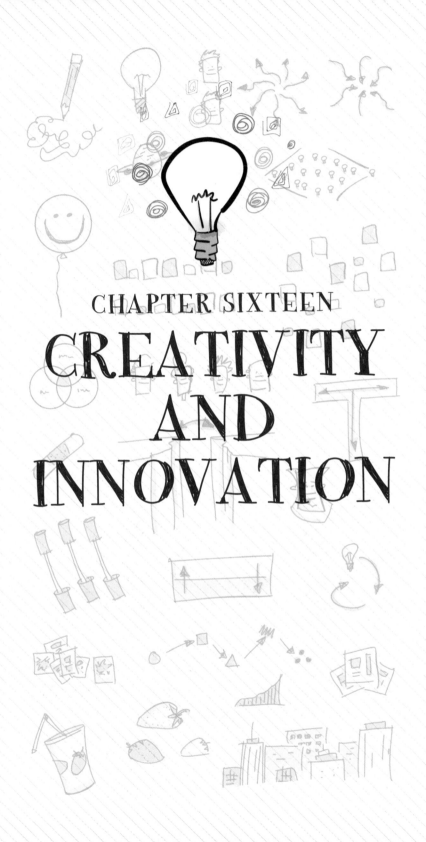

CHAPTER SIXTEEN

CREATIVITY AND INNOVATION

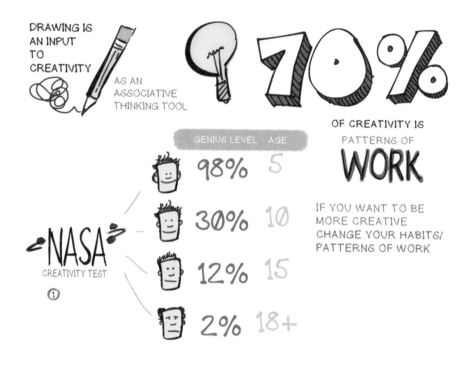

DRAWING IS
AN INPUT
TO
CREATIVITY

AS AN
ASSOCIATIVE
THINKING TOOL

70%

OF CREATIVITY IS
PATTERNS OF

WORK

NASA
CREATIVITY TEST
①

GENIUS LEVEL	AGE
98%	5
30%	10
12%	15
2%	18+

IF YOU WANT TO BE
MORE CREATIVE
CHANGE YOUR HABITS/
PATTERNS OF WORK

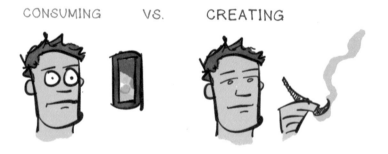

CONSUMING   VS.   CREATING

The problem today is most people spend time CONSUMING versus CREATING. Make a real commitment to start creating. It will benefit both your personal and professional life.

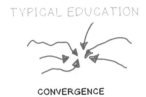

CONVERGENCE

CONFORMITY, ONE DESTINATION

DIVERGENCE

CURIOSITY, EXPLORATION

When brainstorming, the game is all about getting out as many ideas as possible. Crazy ideas. Infeasible ideas. Just get them all out there. Idea generation is about divergence. As tempting as it can be, don't critique any ideas until they are all out there.

Once you have done that, it is time to filter the ideas down (convergence). Put your business hat on and throw out bad ideas. Remember, the only way to get down to a great idea is to start with divergence first, and then convergence.

---

① ②

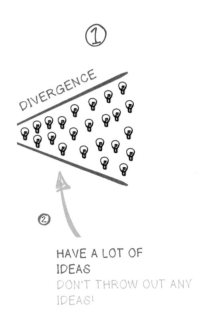

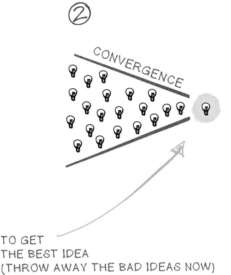

HAVE A LOT OF IDEAS
DON'T THROW OUT ANY IDEAS!

TO GET THE BEST IDEA
(THROW AWAY THE BAD IDEAS NOW)

BREAK THE
STATUS QUO   ASSOCIATIVE   NEW IDEAS
                    THINKING

CRITICAL ESSENCE
OF CREATIVITY

First, think outside the box. Then associate your thoughts with things you have observed or experienced. This is the essence of creativity. Always be filling your "card catalog" with experiences and knowledge. Then take those cards and put them together in different combinations.

KNOWLEDGE RECOMBINATION

EXPERIENCES CREATE NEW PERCEPTS IN OUR MIND

CREATIVES ARE HAPPY BECAUSE THEY ARE ALWAYS FILLING THEIR CARD CATALOG

CREATE CREATIVITY

① FILL YOUR CARD CATALOG

② COMBINE CARDS
- DELIBERATE RECOMBO
- SERENDIPITY FAVORS THE PREPARED MIND
(MIND IS ON THE PROBLEM)

③ FIND NEW CREATIVE IDEAS

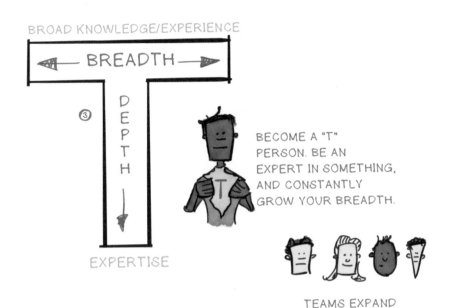

BROAD KNOWLEDGE/EXPERIENCE

← BREADTH →

③ DEPTH

EXPERTISE

BECOME A "T" PERSON. BE AN EXPERT IN SOMETHING, AND CONSTANTLY GROW YOUR BREADTH.

TEAMS EXPAND BREADTH

Teams are critical to expanding your breadth. Include people who are different than you. This helps expand your idea pool dramatically. You can use these associative thinking methods in a team or individually — but try to leverage teams as much as possible.

ASSOCIATIVE
THINKING
METHODS

TWILIGHT THINKING
LOOSE THINKING

BRAINSTORMING
PROPERLY

MINDMAPPING
NON-LINEAR CONNECTIONS

IDEA LOG

SIX THINKING HATS

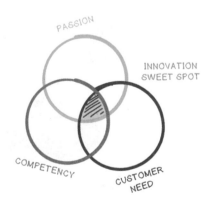

PASSION

INNOVATION
SWEET SPOT

COMPETENCY

CUSTOMER NEED

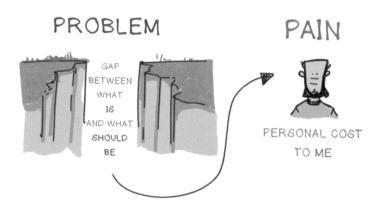

PROBLEM

GAP
BETWEEN
WHAT
IS
AND WHAT
SHOULD
BE

PAIN

PERSONAL COST
TO ME

You may have a great idea that solves a huge problem — but if people don't care, they won't buy it. It could even be a lifesaving device.

"Pain" is personal. Personal Pain causes People to Pay.

PAIN

Any problem or unmet need that people will pay to solve

YOU KNOW YOU HAVE A GOOD IDEA WHEN **CUSTOMERS LIGHT UP** WHEN YOU SHOW THEM

When solving any kind of problem, dive into the complexity. When you are providing the end solution, make it incredibly simple (elegant). Elegant solutions beat out non-elegant solutions 2–4x.

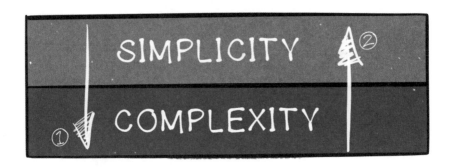

Systematic Inventive Thinking (SIT)④ is a technique to take existing products and create new innovations from them by applying 5 different thinking models.

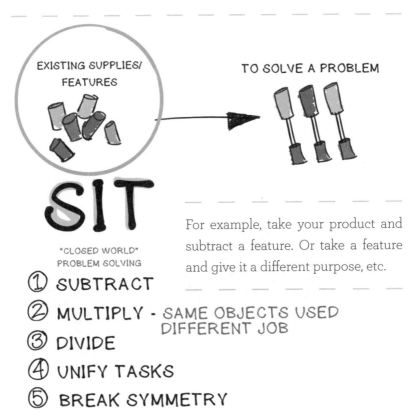

EXISTING SUPPLIES/ FEATURES

TO SOLVE A PROBLEM

SIT

"CLOSED WORLD" PROBLEM SOLVING

For example, take your product and subtract a feature. Or take a feature and give it a different purpose, etc.

① SUBTRACT

② MULTIPLY - SAME OBJECTS USED DIFFERENT JOB

③ DIVIDE

④ UNIFY TASKS

⑤ BREAK SYMMETRY

Creativity is an evolutionary process. Starting with the vision (on day 1), ideas are tested, tweaked, and tested again. Through the process, new knowledge is gained and the product is refined to a point where it finally meets the vision and can be launched for real. A key in the process is to be nimble and flexible — adapting to new information and data.

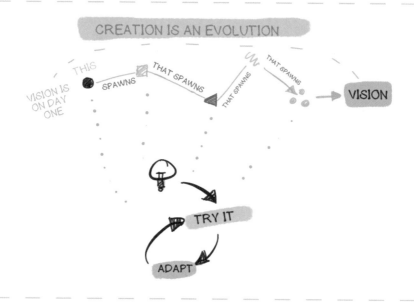

Guest Speaker: Michael Lee. ⑤

Spend time on soft costs (planning, ideating). Most companies invest very little in soft costs, which can be detrimental once a (product, theme park, etc.) is launched.

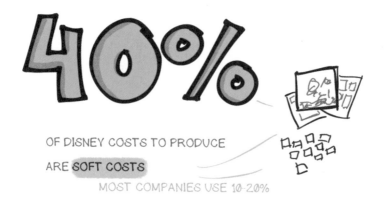

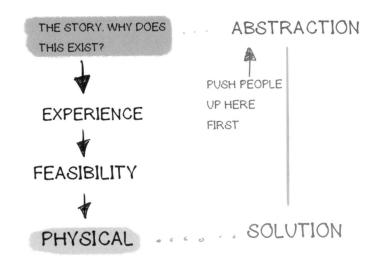

THE STORY. WHY DOES THIS EXIST? ... ABSTRACTION

↓

EXPERIENCE

PUSH PEOPLE UP HERE FIRST

↓

FEASIBILITY

↓

PHYSICAL .... SOLUTION

People always want to jump to solutions. STOP. Bring people back to abstraction — what is the story? Why does the product exist? Then create the experience in your mind's eye.

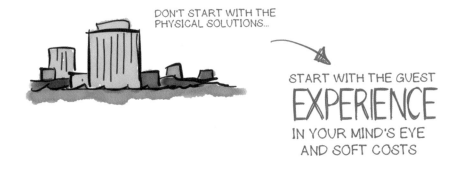

DON'T START WITH THE PHYSICAL SOLUTIONS...

START WITH THE GUEST

EXPERIENCE

IN YOUR MIND'S EYE AND SOFT COSTS

Of course, before you create it you need to look at the numbers and do a feasibility study. If it makes business sense, THEN you start working on the solution.

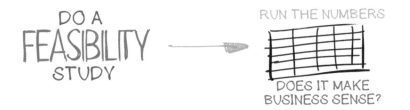

DO A FEASIBILITY STUDY

RUN THE NUMBERS

DOES IT MAKE BUSINESS SENSE?

You can't talk about innovation without talking about Harvard business professor Clayton Christensen. The guy is a genius. He has a masterful theory called the "Job to Be Done."[6]

JOB TO BE DONE

A fast food chain wanted to sell more milkshakes. They did market research and spent a lot of money to learn everything about their target customer.

MALE

20-45

They did surveys and focus groups. Then they enhanced their milkshakes by refining the recipe, brought in their customers, and they liked it!

BETTER BERRIES

SMOOTHER SHAKE

NO increase in sales!

45% of milkshakes were purchased in the morning.

Given this insight they started stopping drivers as they were going through the drive-through and asking "why" they were buying the milkshake. They learned that the customers wanted something that would occupy them while they commuted to work and kept them full until lunch. That was the JOB TO BE DONE that they hired the milkshake for.

IT WASN'T UNTIL THEY UNDERSTOOD WHY THE CUSTOMER BOUGHT THE SHAKE (JOB TO BE DONE) THAT THEY INCREASED SALES 7x.

SALES
7x!

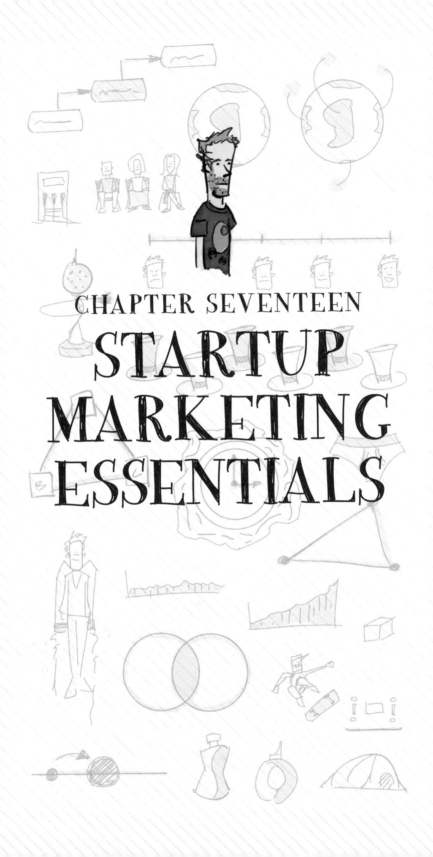

CHAPTER SEVENTEEN
STARTUP MARKETING ESSENTIALS

This course is all about finding a good idea, sharpening the competitive angle, and making it profitable. This simple model took 20+ years to perfect.

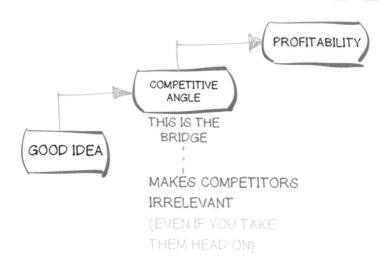

How to create a good idea

TAKE BORING PRODUCTS

AND
MAKE THEM FUN

REINVENT
PRODUCT EXPERIENCE
THE WORLD AROUND YOU

WAYS TO FIND GREAT IDEAS

1. **SOLVE EVERYDAY PAIN**
   Look around. What are people struggling with?

2. **RIDE THE WAVE OF INTEREST**
   What is popular right now? Leverage it.

3. **STRETCH OR ENTERTAIN TO THE EXTREME**
   Take your idea and go to the extreme! For some reason things taken to the extreme are money makers.

4. **BUILD ON A CORE PRODUCT**
   Look at the most common products, find their core, and make them the BEST or MOST FUN. Double down!

5. **COOL HUNTING**
   What's most profitable in other countries that we aren't doing here? Find it and bring it over.

HOW TO KNOW IF YOU HAVE A GOOD IDEA
TEST PERSONAL CONNECTION

WOW
FACTOR

SHOW PEOPLE THE PRODUCT

CONDUCT FOCUS GROUPS

"WOW"

"NICE. GOOD JOB."

ON A SCALE OF 0 (IDEA STINKS) TO 10 (HERE'S MY CREDIT CARD!), WHAT WOULD YOU RATE THIS?

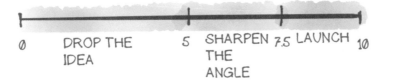

0   DROP THE IDEA   5   SHARPEN THE ANGLE   7.5   LAUNCH   10

STEPS TO CONDUCT
FOCUS GROUPS

SCREENING QUESTION

(TO MAKE SURE THE GROUP REPRESENTS TARGET)

"DO YOU USE (SIMILAR PRODUCT CATEGORY)?"

DO THE 6 THINKING HATS ①

WHITE
State the facts for the focus group. This isn't the time for critiques, just Q & A.

RED
Ask on a scale of 1-10 whether or not they would purchase it.

YELLOW
Perceived benefits or positive support for the product.

BLACK
Perceived shortcomings of the product. This is the time for them to be negative.

GREEN
Ideas for improving the product.

BLUE
Summarize the process and learnings from the thinking hat exercise.

QUESTIONS TO ASK FOR
NEW PRODUCTS

ORDERED
BY MOJO

1. IS IT UNIQUE?
2. IS THERE A LARGE ADDRESSABLE NEED?
3. DOES IT DOMINATE A SPECIFIC USAGE SITUATION?
4. IS ITS DISTINCTION AND/OR (square watermelon) BENEFIT EASY TO SEE?
5. IS THERE QUANTITATIVE EVIDENCE OF PRODUCT SUPERIORITY?

Each of these questions is ordered by mojo (importance).

IS IT A PAIN? — OR ▶ CAN IT GET PEOPLE
TALKING?

WHAT ABOUT YOUR PRODUCT WILL

GET PEOPLE TALKING?

The competitive angle

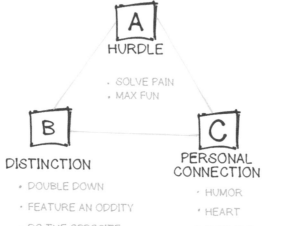

A
HURDLE
- SOLVE PAIN
- MAX FUN

B
DISTINCTION
- DOUBLE DOWN
- FEATURE AN ODDITY
- DO THE OPPOSITE

C
PERSONAL CONNECTION
- HUMOR
- HEART
- SUPPORT A CAUSE
- BABIES, KIDS, PETS

(HOW YOU MESSAGE & BUILD A BRAND)

The competitive angle has 3 parts. A: helps someone get over a hurdle, B: is distinct, C: creates a positive personal connection. Once you have a good idea, it is time to sharpen the competitive angle to make it profitable.

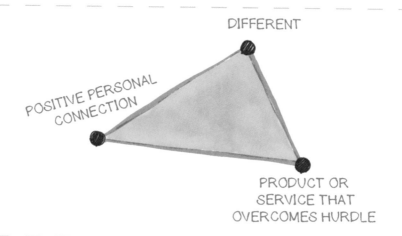

DIFFERENT

POSITIVE PERSONAL CONNECTION

PRODUCT OR SERVICE THAT OVERCOMES HURDLE

Sometimes your angle will look unbalanced like this. Work to balance it out by sharpening the dull points.

ELEMENTS OF DIFFERENTNESS

* REMARKABLE BOTTOM-UP TACTIC

→ **DOUBLE DOWN**
"YOU'RE CHEAP? WE ARE TWICE AS CHEAP!"
BETTER, FASTER, CHEAPER
GO DOUBLE BETTER, FASTER, CHEAPER

→ **DO THE OPPOSITE**
MILK→ ALMOND SILK "NOT MILK"

→ **FEATURE AN ODDITY**
SQUATTY POTTY

The cow patty clock is a great example of a product that featured an odd-ity and doubled down. The only limitation they had was in creating the supply. Cows only poop so much.

UPC UNIQUE PRODUCT CLAIM

COW PATTY CLOCK

The jet pack water ride started as a product to clean the sides of large ships. Sales were level. They took that idea, sharpened the angle by making it unique, and targeted for a different situation. Sales skyrocketed (no pun intended).

ORIGINALLY DESIGNED TO CLEAN SHIPS

SALES

ENTERTAINMENT

SALES

IF YOU ALREADY HAVE A PRODUCT, GET CREATIVE ON THE POSSIBLE SITUATIONS

Positive personal connections are critical. Be careful of creating a product that elicits a negative personal connection.

DISPOSABLE UNDERWEAR

WOULD YOU BUY THEM? NO? WHY?

"WHEN I PUT THESE, ON, THEY MAKE ME FEEL WEIRD."

NEGATIVE EMOTIONAL CONNECTION

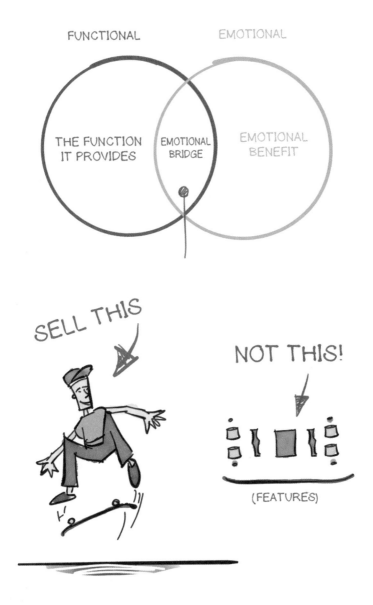

A lot of companies focus on selling features rather than taking a much more effective approach selling benefits. Show potential customers the idea and appeal to the emotions, creating a positive personal connection.

Get creative on different usage situations for your product. An apron company thought their product was for one situation when they discovered that their audience really wanted to feel cute. The process looks something like this:

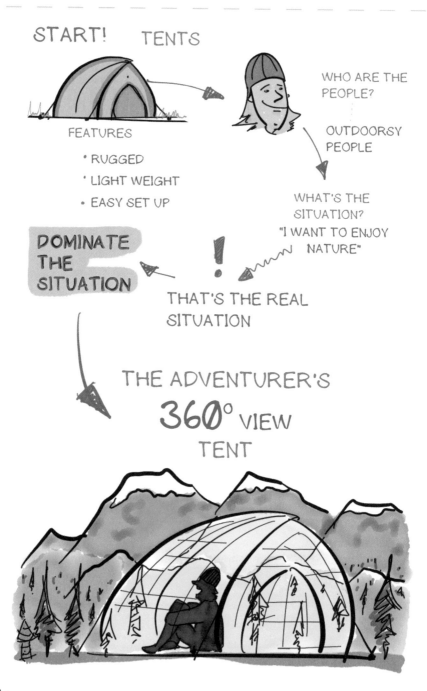

START! TENTS

FEATURES

* RUGGED
* LIGHT WEIGHT
• EASY SET UP

WHO ARE THE PEOPLE?

OUTDOORSY PEOPLE

WHAT'S THE SITUATION?

"I WANT TO ENJOY NATURE"

DOMINATE THE SITUATION

!

THAT'S THE REAL SITUATION

THE ADVENTURER'S

360° VIEW

TENT

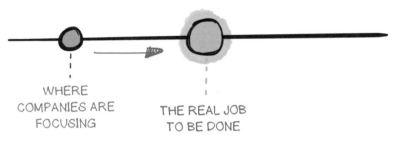

THE REAL SITUATION

WHERE COMPANIES ARE FOCUSING

THE REAL JOB TO BE DONE

USE FOCUS GROUPS TO DISCOVER THE REAL SITUATION

The reality is, most customers are using your product for reasons other than you originally thought. Doing focus groups will help you flesh out how they are using it, which will help you dominate that usage situation.

DISCOVER the SITUATION
FIRST
AND IT WILL DETERMINE THE FEATURE SET

Take your product idea and create a table with target customers on the left and at least 10 different usage situations along the top. Find the most profitable customer with the most powerful situation and focus there. Although it is tempting to focus on all of them, you need to focus on ONLY ONE.

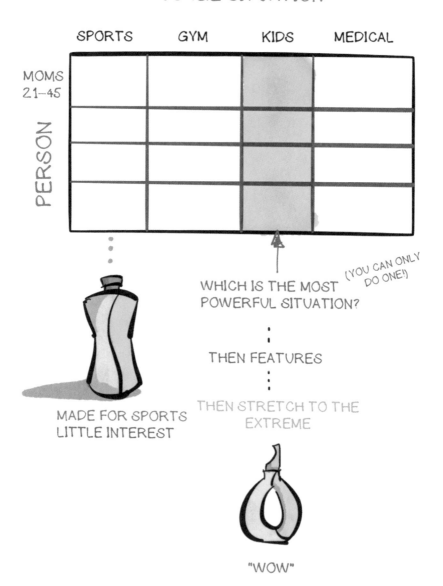

USAGE SITUATION

SPORTS · GYM · KIDS · MEDICAL

PERSON

MOMS 21–45

WHICH IS THE MOST POWERFUL SITUATION? (YOU CAN ONLY DO ONE!)

THEN FEATURES

THEN STRETCH TO THE EXTREME

MADE FOR SPORTS LITTLE INTEREST

"WOW"

Situation Statement
Creating a situation statement will help focus your efforts

[Target customer] wants to [resolve pain-point / enjoy fun-point] but can't because of [hurdle]; [product] gets [target customer] over the [hurdle] by [value innovation].

YOU ARE LOOKING FOR AN

STRATEGY

THE BEST PRODUCT IS ONE WHERE YOU KNOW WHO IS GOING TO BUY THE COMPANY BEFORE YOU EVEN START

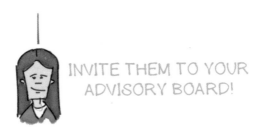

INVITE THEM TO YOUR ADVISORY BOARD!

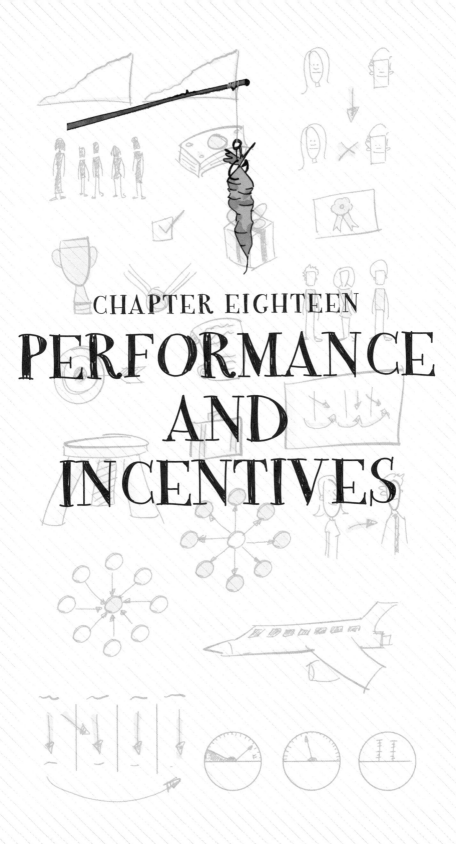

CHAPTER EIGHTEEN

PERFORMANCE AND INCENTIVES

If a quarterback is about to get sacked, should he throw the ball away or just take the sack? The owner wants him to throw it away so that the QB doesn't risk an injury, but the QB wants to take the sack so he has better passing completion stats. How do you reconcile the two? That is what this chapter is all about.

WHY NOT INCENTIVIZE BASED ON WINS?
CAN'T CONTROL IT
"IF I CAN'T CONTROL IT, WHY BOTHER?"

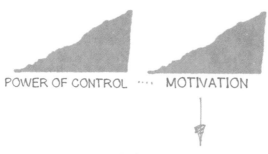

POWER OF CONTROL ···· MOTIVATION

PRIMED FOR INCENTIVES
IF THERE IS A MOTIVATION PROBLEM
THERE COULD BE A CONTROL PROBLEM

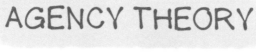

AGENCY THEORY

①

CEO   EMPLOYEE
PRINCIPAL   AGENT

SELF UTILITY
MAXIMIZING
(SELF-SERVING)

The agency theory states that the agent will want to maximize utility for one's own benefit. Goal incongruence is when the principal and the agent's goals don't align.

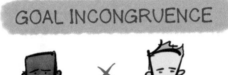

The reality is that people want the most amount of money while doing the least amount of work. This course is about creating structure and incentives that align the business objectives with the motivations of employees.

MANAGEMENT CONTROL SYSTEMS
EXIST FOR AGENCY PROBLEMS

INCENTIVES

BUSINESS GOALS

ORGANIZATIONAL ARCHITECTURE ②

DECISION RIGHTS

PERFORMANCE MEASURES

INCENTIVE SYSTEMS

YOU NEED ALL **3**, AND THEY ALL ARE EQUAL IN IMPORTANCE

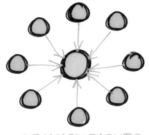
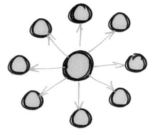

DECISION RIGHTS
CENTRALIZED

DECISION RIGHTS
DECENTRALIZED

ANY SHIFT IN
THE ORGANIZATION
REQUIRES A
SHIFT IN MEASUREMENT
&
INCENTIVES

PRINCIPAL

AGENT

PRINCIPAL
EMPLOYS AGENT
TO MANAGE AN
ASSET ON THEIR
BEHALF

AGENT HAS DECISION
MAKING RIGHTS

MEASURED ON X
FOR HIS PLANT

MEASURED ON X
FOR HIS PLANT

MEASURED ON X
FOR HIS PLANT

INCENTIVIZED TO BE SILOED EVEN THOUGH
IT DOES NOT BENEFIT THE ORGANIZATION

PERFORMANCE
MEASURES

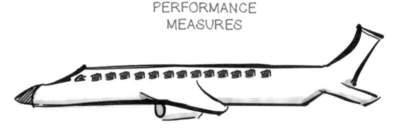

FUEL　SPEED　ALTITUDE

YOU DON'T JUST FOCUS ON
ONE MEASURE

BALANCED
SCORECARD

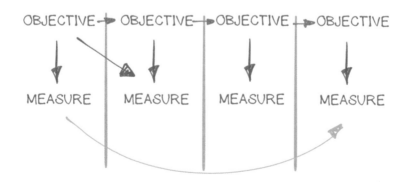

OBJECTIVE → OBJECTIVE → OBJECTIVE → OBJECTIVE

MEASURE　MEASURE　MEASURE　MEASURE

BALANCED
SCORECARD ③
EXAMPLE

Internal Processes Perspective	Learning & Growth Perspective	Customers' Perspective	Financial Perspective
Operational Excellence	Motivated Workforce	Delight the Customer	Increase Revenues
↓	↓	↓	↓
Reduced Inventory	Employee Surveys	Customer Satisfaction	Sales

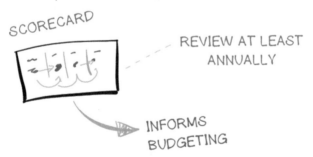

SCORECARD

REVIEW AT LEAST ANNUALLY

INFORMS BUDGETING

WHAT GETS MEASURED

GETS DONE

Just watch out for surrogation. This is when the measure itself becomes the end. For example, measuring managers on whether or not they have 1:1s with their team. The purpose is to help their team members, but the quality of those meetings could go downhill if they feel they just need to check the box.

CHAPTER NINETEEN

GLOBAL MANAGEMENT

Global management is about taking your product or business out to the world while being aware of the local needs and cultures in order to increase your chances of success.

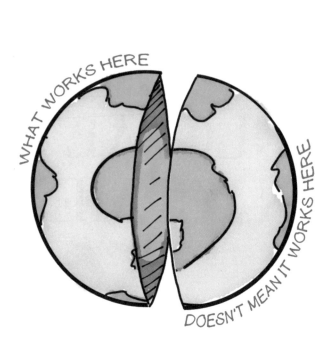

WHAT WORKS HERE

DOESN'T MEAN IT WORKS HERE

CULTURAL DIFFERENCES, PREFERENCES, NEEDS

IT'S NOT JUST GEOGRAPHY THAT CAUSES DISTANCE

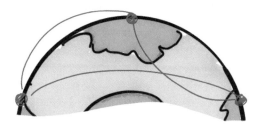

Companies have made many botched attempts at opening new markets around the world only to discover that their product doesn't truly meet the market's needs or wants. Although tempting to jump into markets like China, doing the proper legwork to understand the cultural differences in attitudes, behaviors, expectations, and values will go a long way.

CULTURE

ATTITUDES	LEARNED	BY A GROUP OF PEOPLE
BEHAVIORS	SHARED	
EXPECTATIONS	TRANSMITTED	
VALUES		

CAGE
DISTANCE FRAMEWORK ①

Distance is created by more than just geography. When looking at your international strategy the CAGE framework will help you navigate potential pitfalls.

C ULTURAL DIFFERENCES

What are the different languages? Ethnicities? Religions? Values? Norms?

A DMINISTRATIVE DIFFERENCES

What is the political landscape? What is the legal system? Currency?

GEOGRAPHIC DIFFERENCES

What is the physical distance between countries? Time zones? Climates?

ECONOMIC DIFFERENCES

What are the differences between the rich and poor? What is the infrastructure? Natural/financial resources?

CULTURAL	ADMINISTRATIVE	GEOGRAPHIC	ECONOMIC

Now you can easily put the answers to these questions in a table for reference when planning and sharing your strategy. Accounting for these four areas will save you much trouble down the road as you look to expand your business.

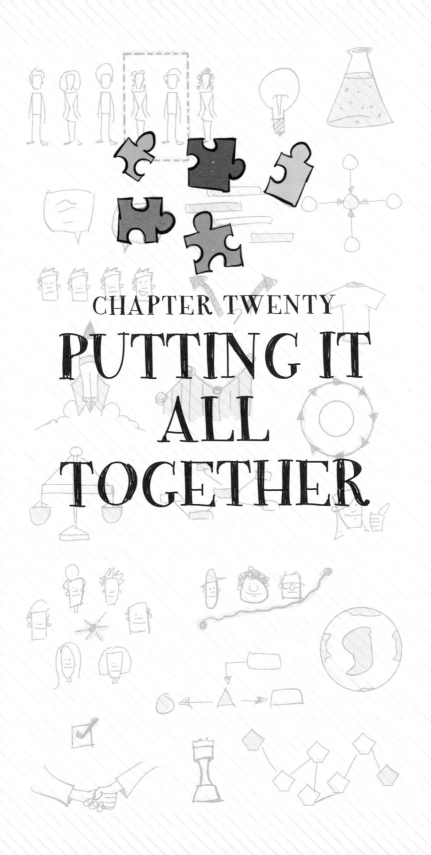

CHAPTER TWENTY

PUTTING IT ALL TOGETHER

Wow, that was a lot of stuff. Let's see how it all fits together for a new business venture. Hopefully this reference guide can help you along your own business journey!

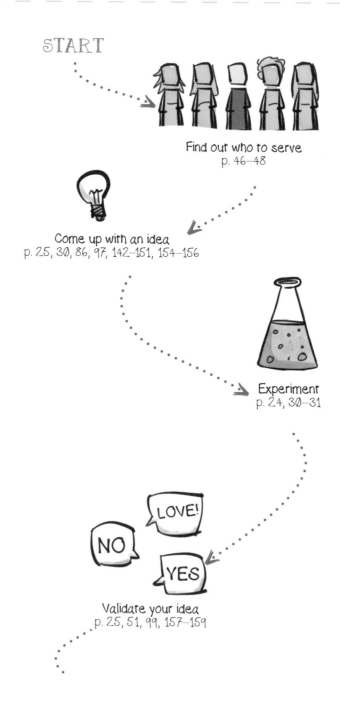

START

Find out who to serve
p. 46–48

Come up with an idea
p. 25, 30, 86, 97, 142–151, 154–156

Experiment
p. 24, 30–31

LOVE!

NO

YES

Validate your idea
p. 25, 51, 99, 157–159

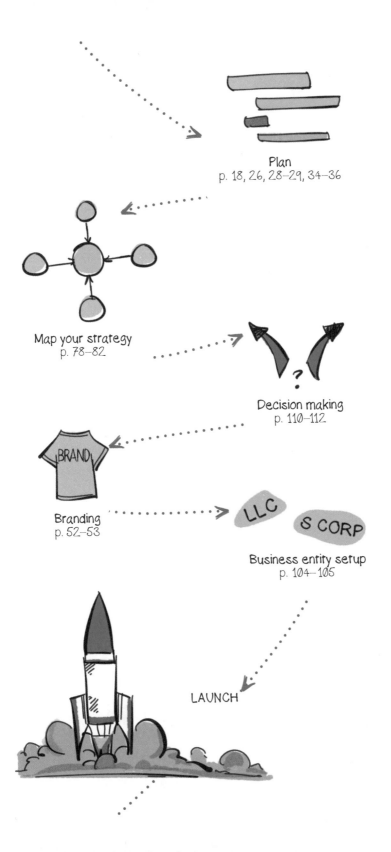

Plan
p. 18, 26, 28–29, 34–36

Map your strategy
p. 78–82

Decision making
p. 110–112

BRAND

Branding
p. 52–53

LLC

S CORP

Business entity setup
p. 104–105

LAUNCH

NEW!

Marketing
p. 46–49, 163

Measure & diagnose
p. 12–17

Refine your product & marketing
p. 49–51, 154, 160–162, 164–167

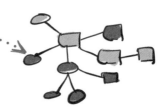

Problem solving
p. 120–122

Leadership
p. 2–5, 136–139

Ethics
p. 90–93

Building teams
p. 6–9, 62–63

Performance improvement
p. 170–175

Employee retention
p. 64–67

Managing change
p. 124–131

Grow and invest in the business
p. 25, 51, 99, 157–159

Global expansion
p. 178–181

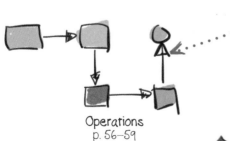

Operations
p. 56–59

Negotiations
p. 70–75

Closing Thoughts

Feeling smarter? Good. You've gained insights. You've made connections. You've learned new things. Now it's time to apply them.

70% of learning is experiential and now it is up to you. Try the concepts and frameworks you learned. What worked? What didn't? What could be improved?

Learning never stops. Socrates lived over 2,000 years ago (469-399 B.C.) and he knew what he was talking about. Dig deep, ask "why?," challenge, ask questions, and then DO. You will understand the whole picture rather than fragments. You are an artist with many canvases ready to be filled by your intellectual curiosity and discovery. If you can "sketchnote" some of them along the way, bonus points.

If you take and apply just one idea in this book, try it out, learn, and grow, all the hours spent on this book will be worth it.

Thank you for buying and reading this book. I look forward to hearing your experiences and insights as you apply these concepts. Feel free to reach me on Instagram: @visualmba.

Kind regards,
Jason Barron

REFERENCES

Chapter 1

1. Ulrich, Dave, and Norm Smallwood. "Building a Leadership Brand." *Harvard Business Review* (July–August 2007).
2. Ulrich, Dave, and Norm Smallwood. "Five Steps to Building Your Personal Leadership Brand." *Harvard Business Review* (December 2007).
3. Goman, Carol K. "Seven Seconds to Make a First Impression." *Forbes* (February 2011). https://www.forbes.com/sites/carolkinseygoman/2011/02/13/seven-sec onds-to-make-a-first-impression/#4d31f1dd2722.
4. Pink, Daniel H. *Drive: The Surprising Truth About What Motivates Us.* New York: Riverhead Books, 2009.
5. Lindquist, Rusty. "Finding Your Own Personal Sweet Spot." *Life Engineering blog* (August 2008). https://life.engineering/finding-your-own-personal-sweet-spot/.
6. Professor Sumantra Ghoshal. Speech at World Economic Forum in Davos, Switzerland (n.d.). https://www.youtube.com/watch?v=UUddgE8rI0E.
7. Schwartz, Tony, and Catherine McCarthy. "Manage Your Energy, Not Your Time." *Harvard Business Review* (October 2007).
8. Dyer, William G., W. Gibb Dyer, Jr., and Jeffrey H. Dyer. *Team Building: Proven Strategies for Improving Team Performance* (4th ed.). San Francisco: Jossey-Bass, 2007.

Chapter 3

1. Ideo. "How to Prototype a New Business." Blog entry. https://www.ideou.com/blogs/inspiration/how-to-prototype-a-new-business.
2. Mankin, Eric. "Can You Spot the Sure Winner?" *Harvard Business Review* (July 2004).
3. Levy, Steven. *The Perfect Thing: How the iPod Shuffles Commerce, Culture, and Coolness.* New York: Simon & Schuster, 2007.
4. https://dschool.stanford.edu/resources.

Chapter 4

1. Monte Swain. "The Management Process." In "Management Accounting and Cost Concepts," Chapter 15 in W. Steve Albrecht et al., *Accounting: Concepts and Applications.* Boston: Cengage Learning, 2007.

Chapter 6

1. Reynolds, Thomas J., and Jonathan Gutman. "Laddering Theory, Method, Analysis, and Interpretation." *Journal of Advertising Research* (February/March 1988).
2. Sinek, Simon. "How Great Leaders Inspire Action." TED Talk given in Puget Sound, Washington, September 2009. https://www.ted.com/talks/simon_sinek_how_great_leaders_inspire_action.

Chapter 7

1. Gray, Ann E., and James Leonard. "Process Fundamentals." Harvard Business School Background Note 696–023, September 1995. (Revised July 2016.)

Chapter 8

1. Hackman, J. Richard, and Greg R. Oldham. (1975.) "Development of the Job Diagnostic Survey." *Journal of Applied Psychology* 60, (2): 159–170.
2. Herzberg, Frederick. "The Motivation-Hygiene Concept and Problems of Manpower." *Personnel Administrator* 27 (January–February 1964): 3–7.
3. Dyer, William G., W. Gibb Dyer, Jr., and Jeffrey H. Dyer. *Team Building: Proven Strategies for Improving Team Performance* (4th ed.). San Francisco: Jossey-Bass, 2007.

Chapter 9

1. Forsyth, D. R. *Group Dynamics*. Belmont, MA: Wadsworth, Cengage Learning, 2010, 2006.
2. Fisher, Roger, Bruce Patton, and William Ury. *Getting to Yes: Negotiating Agreement Without Giving In*. Rev. ed. New York: Penguin Books, 2011.
3. Diamond, Stuart. Getting More: *How You Can Negotiate to Succeed in Work and Life*. New York: Crown Business, 2012.

Chapter 10

1. Porter, Michael. "How Competitive Forces Shape Strategy." *Harvard Business Review* (March 1979).
2. Porter, Michael. "What Is Strategy." *Harvard Business Review* (November/December 1996).
3. Barney, J. B., and W. S. Hesterly. "VRIO Framework." In *Strategic Management and Competitive Advantage*. Upper Saddle River, NJ: Pearson, 2010, pp. 68–86.
4. Kim, W. C., and R. Mauborgne. *Blue Ocean Strategy: How to Create Uncontested Market Space and Make the Competition Irrelevant*. Boston: Harvard Business Review Press, 2005.

Chapter 12

1. Drucker, Peter F. *Innovation and Entrepreneurship*. New York: HarperBusiness, 2006.

Chapter 13

1. Hammond, John S., Ralph L. Keeney, and Howard Raiffa. *Smart Choices: A Practical Guide to Making Better Decisions*. Boston: Harvard Business Review Press, 2015.

2. Kahneman, Daniel. *Thinking, Fast and Slow*. New York: Farrar, Straus and Giroux, 2013.

3. Tversky, Amos; Kahneman, Daniel (1973). "Availability: A heuristic for judging frequency and probability." *Cognitive Psychology* 5 (2): 207–232.

4. Kahneman, Daniel; Tversky, Amos (1972). "Subjective probability: A judgment of representativeness." *Cognitive Psychology* 3 (3): 430–454.

5. Kahneman, Daniel; Tversky, Amos (1979). "Prospect Theory: An Analysis of Decision under Risk." *Econometrica* 47 (2): 263.

6. Tversky, A.; Kahneman, D. (1974). "Judgment under Uncertainty: Heuristics and Biases." *Science* 185 (4157): 1124–1131.

7. Lichtenstein, Sarah; Fischhoff, Baruch; Phillips, Lawrence D. "Calibration of probabilities: The state of the art to 1980." In Kahneman, Daniel; Slovic, Paul; Tversky, Amos. *Judgment Under Uncertainty: Heuristics and Biases*. Cambridge, U.K.: Cambridge University Press, 1982, pp. 306–334.

8. Kunda, Z. (1990.) "The case for motivated reasoning." *Psychological Bulletin* 108 (3), 480–498.

Chapter 14

1. Doran, G. T. (1981.) "There's a S.M.A.R.T. way to write management's goals and objectives." *Management Review*, AMA FORUM 70 (11): 35–36.

2. Lewin, Kurt. (1947.) "Frontiers in Group Dynamics: Concept, Method and Reality in Social Science; Social Equilibria and Social Change." *Human Relations* 1: 5–41.

3. Bridges, William. *Managing Transitions*. Boston: Nicholas Brealey Publishing, 2009.

Chapter 16

1. Ainsworth-Land, George T., and Beth Jarman. *Breakpoint and Beyond: Mastering the Future – Today*. Champaign, IL: HarperBusiness, 1992.

2. Gray, Dave, Sunni Brown, and James Macanufo. *Gamestorming*. Sebastopol, CA: O'Reilly Media, 2010.

3. "The hunt is on for the Renaissance Man of computing," in *The Independent*, September 17, 1991.

4. Created by Ginadi Filkovsky, Jacob Goldenberg, and Roni Horowitz.

5. Michael Lee, http://mldworldwide.com.

6. Clayton Christensen et al. "Know Your Customers' "Jobs to be Done."" *Harvard Business Review* (September 2016).

Chapter 17

1. de Bono, Edward. *Six Thinking Hats: An Essential Approach to Business Management*. Boston: Little, Brown & Company, 1985.

Chapter 18

1. Eisenhardt, K. (1989.) "Agency theory: An assessment and review." *Academy of Management Review* 14 (1): 57–74.
2. Gupta, Mahendra R., Antonio Davila, and Richard J. Palmer. https://olin.wustl.edu/EN-US/Faculty-Research/research/Pages/performance-effects-organizational-architecture.aspx.
3. Kaplan, Robert S; Norton, D. P. *The Balanced Scorecard: Translating Strategy into Action.* Boston: Harvard Business Review Press, 1996.

Chapter 19

1. Framework created by Pankaj Ghemawat, http://www.ghemawat.com/.

Acknowledgments

I want to give a special thanks to my amazing, supportive, patient, strong, beautiful wife, Jackie. She always encouraged me and never complained once through my entire MBA program (and while I was creating this book), all the while raising our five children.

I also want to thank the incredible classmates I learned so much from and who will be friends for life.

A huge thank you to all the top-notch professors who made my MBA experience as challenging and rewarding as it was: Curtis LeBaron and Michael Thompson (Leadership), Jim Stice (Corporate Financial Reporting), Nile Hatch (Entrepreneurial Management, Creativity and Innovation), Monte Swain (Managerial Accounting), Colby Wright (Business Finance), Glenn Christensen and Michael Swenson (Marketing), Daniel Snow and Cindy Wallin (Operations Management), John Bingham and Peter Madsen (Strategic HR Management), Bruce Money (Business Negotiations, Global Management), Mark Hansen (Strategy, Strategic Thinking), Brad Agle (Business Ethics), Jim Brau (Entrepreneurial Finance), Bill Tayler and Doug Prawitt (Judgment and Decision Making), Paul Godfrey (The General Manager's Role), Gary Rhoads and David Whitlark (Startup Marketing Essentials), and finally Steve Smith and Bill Tayler (Performance and Incentives).

I want to thank my friend, Ben Norris, who introduced me to sketchnotes, my mother, Faith, who always taught me to present my best work no matter how small a project, my awesome brother Matt for his feedback and support, my agent David Fugate, and the incredible team at Houghton Mifflin Harcourt.

About the Author

Jason Barron, MBA, is a creative leader focused on digital product strategy and user experience. He is a founding partner of the startup LowestMed that was acquired by RetailMeNot in 2018, and currently works for a large nonprofit organization on digital products that serve millions of users around the world.

Jason's grandparents, Donald and Dorothy Colley, both attended Harvard University and instilled in him the importance of education at a young age. He received his Masters of Business Administration from Brigham Young University in 2017 and his Bachelors degree from Southern Virginia University in 2007.

Jason has the unique ability to simplify complexity and infuse creativity in business strategy. His Kickstarter for the original rendition of this book raised over 1,000% of his goal in 28 days from over 40 countries around the world.

Jason is known to set stretch goals (literally). Never having been able to touch his toes, he filmed the journey and met his goal after 41 days. His video has since received several million views after being shared by George Takei (*Star Trek*) as well as Yahoo and MSN news.

Jason currently lives in Salt Lake City, Utah with his wife and five children. Find out more about Jason at jasonbarron.com